Shortcuts to Making Fabulous Desserts

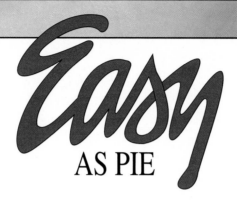

Easy
AS PIE

With the simple recipes, timesaving techniques, and super shortcuts in this exciting volume, you can enjoy fabulous desserts anytime! Whether you need something sensational for an elegant affair or a quick treat for the kids, Easy As Pie will guide you to great pies, cakes, cookies, and more in a flash! We've taken advantage of convenience items such as cake and pudding mixes, canned pie fillings, and refrigerated doughs to create ten taste-tempting collections of the most delicious desserts ever. You'll savor our frozen confections and dreamy creamy desserts. Indulge your family's sweet tooth with extra-easy pies, or take advantage of summer's ripe, juicy harvest with fresh fruit treats. And yes, it really is a piece of cake to bake fabulous oven offerings. When time is especially short, turn to our selections of so-quick sweets or easy sauces — many of which can be prepared using the microwave! Because children want their snacks fast and fun, we've included lots of speedy kid pleasers, too. And our no-hassle holiday collection shows you how to sweeten family celebrations all through the year. With Easy As Pie, your desserts will taste like you cooked all day — and only you will know you didn't!

Anne Childs

LEISURE ARTS, INC.
Little Rock, Arkansas

Shortcuts to Making Fabulous Desserts

Easy AS PIE

EDITORIAL STAFF

Vice President and Editor-in-Chief:
Anne Van Wagner Childs
Executive Director: Sandra Graham Case
Executive Editor: Susan Frantz Wiles
Publications Director: Carla Bentley
Creative Art Director: Gloria Bearden
Production Art Director: Melinda Stout

FOODS
Foods Editor: Celia Fahr Harkey, R.D.
Assistant Foods Editor: Jane Kenner Prather
Test Kitchen Home Economist: Rose Glass Klein
Test Kitchen Assistants: Nora Faye Spencer Clift and
Leslie Belote Dunn
Contributing Foods Editors: Linda Adams and
Susan Warren Reeves, R.D.

ART
Book/Magazine Art Director: Diane M. Hugo
Senior Production Artist: Michael A. Spigner
Photography Stylist: Karen Smart Hall

EDITORIAL
Associate Editor: Linda L. Trimble
Senior Editorial Writer: Tammi Williamson Bradley
Editorial Writers: Darla Burdette Kelsay, Debby Carr, and
Cary E. Temple
Editorial Associates: Terri Leming Davidson and
Robyn Sheffield-Edwards
Copy Editor: Laura Lee Weland

ADVERTISING AND DIRECT MAIL
Senior Editor: Tena Kelley Vaughn
Copywriters: Steven M. Cooper, Marla Shivers, and
Marjorie Ann Lacy
Assistant Copywriter: Dixie L. Morris
Designer: Rhonda H. Hestir
Art Director: Jeff Curtis
Production Artists: Linda Lovette Smart and
Leslie Loring Krebs

BUSINESS STAFF

Publisher: Bruce Akin
Vice President, Finance: Tom Siebenmorgen
Vice President, Retail Sales: Thomas L. Carlisle
Retail Sales Director: Richard Tignor
Vice President, Retail Marketing: Pam Stebbins
Retail Customer Services Director: Margaret Sweetin
General Merchandise Manager: Russ Barnett

Distribution Director: Ed M. Strackbein
Executive Director of Marketing and Circulation:
Guy A. Crossley
Circulation Manager: Byron L. Taylor
Print Production Manager: Laura Lockhart
Print Production Coordinator: Nancy Reddick Baker

Library of Congress Catalog Number 95-81737
International Standard Book Number 0-942237-99-4

Table of Contents

TOP IT OFF!..............................90

SPEEDY KID PLEASERS.....................100

NO-HASSLE HOLIDAY TREATS 112

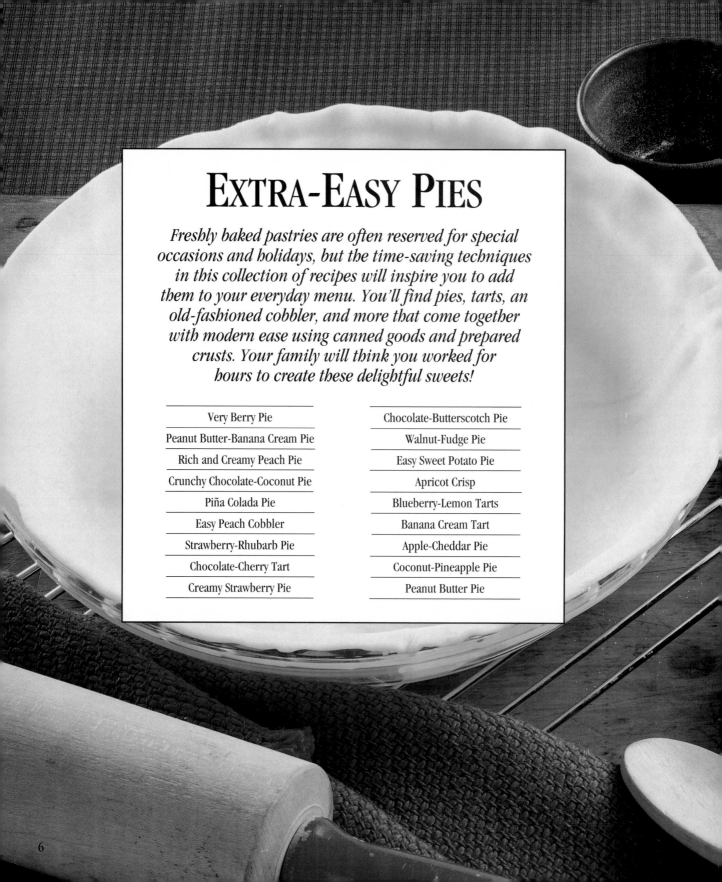

EXTRA-EASY PIES

Freshly baked pastries are often reserved for special occasions and holidays, but the time-saving techniques in this collection of recipes will inspire you to add them to your everyday menu. You'll find pies, tarts, an old-fashioned cobbler, and more that come together with modern ease using canned goods and prepared crusts. Your family will think you worked for hours to create these delightful sweets!

Canned pie filling and frozen berries make Very Berry Pie a triple fruity dessert that's easy to create. The decorative "quilt-block" motif is quick to cut from refrigerated pie crust.

VERY BERRY PIE

- 1 can (21 ounces) cherry pie filling
- 1 can (21 ounces) blueberry pie filling
- 1 package (12 ounces) frozen whole red raspberries, thawed
- 3/4 cup plus 1 tablespoon sugar, divided
- 1/4 teaspoon plus 1/8 teaspoon ground cinnamon, divided
- 1/4 teaspoon orange extract
- 1 package (15 ounces) refrigerated pie crusts, at room temperature

Preheat oven to 400 degrees. For filling, combine pie fillings, raspberries, 3/4 cup sugar, 1/4 teaspoon cinnamon, and orange extract in a large bowl. Place 1 crust in a 9-inch deep-dish pie plate. Pour filling into crust. Cut triangles in center of second crust; pull cut edges back toward center. Place crust over filling; crimp edges. Combine remaining 1 tablespoon sugar and 1/8 teaspoon cinnamon in a small bowl; sprinkle over crust. Bake 45 to 50 minutes or until filling is bubbly and crust is golden brown. If edges of crust brown too quickly, cover with a strip of aluminum foil. Serve warm or transfer to a wire rack to cool.

Yield: about 10 servings

PEANUT BUTTER-BANANA CREAM PIE

- 1/3 cup sifted confectioners sugar
- 1/3 cup crunchy peanut butter
- 1/4 cup plus 2 tablespoons semisweet chocolate mini chips, divided
- 1 purchased graham cracker pie crust (6 ounces)
- 1 1/4 cups milk
- 1 package (3 ounces) vanilla pudding mix
- 1 package (8 ounces) cream cheese, softened
- 2 bananas, sliced

...ombine confectioners sugar, peanut
...er, and 1/4 cup chocolate chips in a
...ll bowl. Lightly press peanut butter
...ture over bottom of crust. In a medium
...epan, combine milk and pudding mix.
...ring constantly, cook over medium heat
...ut 8 minutes or until mixture thickens.
...ove from heat; beat in cream cheese.
...nge banana slices evenly over peanut
...er mixture in crust. Pour pudding
...ture over bananas. Cover and chill about
...ur or until set. To serve, sprinkle with
...aining 2 tablespoons chocolate chips.
...e in an airtight container in refrigerator.
...d: about 8 servings

...CH AND CREAMY PEACH PIE

...4 cup sugar
...2 cup all-purpose flour
...8 teaspoon ground nutmeg
...8 teaspoon salt
...2 cans (16 ounces each) sliced
       peaches, drained
...1 teaspoon almond extract
...1 9-inch unbaked pie crust
...1 cup whipping cream
...2 tablespoons sliced almonds

...reheat oven to 350 degrees. Combine
...ar, flour, nutmeg, and salt in a small
...l; stir in peaches and almond extract.
...on peach mixture into crust. Pour
...pping cream over peach mixture. Bake
...to 55 minutes or until top is lightly
...wned. Sprinkle almonds in center of pie;
...e 5 minutes longer. Serve warm or
...sfer to a wire rack to cool. Store in an
...ight container in refrigerator.
...d: about 8 servings

Sliced almonds add a pleasant surprise to Rich and Creamy Peach Pie (top), a divine dessert that couldn't be easier to make using canned peaches and a purchased pie crust. Layers of chocolaty peanut butter and banana slices are hidden beneath a cream cheese pudding filling in Peanut Butter-Banana Cream Pie.

9

CRUNCHY CHOCOLATE-COCONUT PIE

CRUST

- 1/2 cup semisweet chocolate chips
- 2 tablespoons butter or margarine
- 1 1/2 cups crispy rice cereal
- 1/2 cup flaked coconut

FILLING

- 1 can (8.5 ounces) cream of coconut, chilled
- 1/2 cup milk
- 1 package (3.9 ounces) chocolate fudge instant pudding mix

Coconut to garnish

For crust, place chocolate chips in a medium microwave-safe bowl. Microwave on high power (100%) 1 minute or until chocolate softens. Add butter; stir until smooth. Stir in cereal and coconut until well blended. Lightly press mixture into an ungreased 9-inch pie plate. Cover and chill crust.

For filling, combine cream of coconut and milk in a medium bowl. Add pudding mix; beat until thickened. Pour into chilled crust. Cover and chill about 30 minutes or until set. Garnish with coconut.

Yield: about 8 servings

PIÑA COLADA PIE

- 1 package (3.4 ounces) vanilla instant pudding mix
- 1 1/2 cups liquid piña colada drink mixer, chilled
- 1 package (8 ounces) cream cheese, softened
- 1 can (15 1/4 ounces) pineapple tidbits, drained
- 1/4 cup finely shredded coconut
- 1 purchased graham cracker pie crust (6 ounces)

Kiwi fruit slices to garnish

A crispy rice cereal crust adds texture to Crunchy Chocolate-Coconut Pie (top), a dreamy confection created using instant pudding and cream of coconut. Garnished with kiwi fruit slices, Piña Colada Pie combines a tropical drink mixer with cream cheese, coconut, and pineapple.

The whole family will love Easy Peach Cobbler, an old-fashioned favorite that you can whip up in a jiffy using canned filling. The fruit is spread over the crust, which rises to the top and browns during baking.

n a medium bowl, add pudding mix to
k mixer; beat until thickened. Add
am cheese to pudding mixture; beat until
ooth. Stir in pineapple and coconut.
on into crust. Cover and chill until set.
nish with kiwi fruit slices.

d: about 8 servings

SY PEACH COBBLER

/2 cup butter or margarine, cut into
      pieces
  1 cup sugar

  1 cup all-purpose flour
  2 teaspoons baking powder
 1/2 teaspoon salt
 1/2 teaspoon apple pie spice
 3/4 cup milk
  1 teaspoon almond extract
  1 can (21 ounces) peach
      pie filling

Preheat oven to 350 degrees. Place butter
pieces in a 7 x 11-inch baking dish. Heat in
oven 3 minutes or until butter melts. In a
medium bowl, combine sugar, flour, baking

powder, salt, and apple pie spice. Add milk
and almond extract; stir until well blended.
Pour batter over melted butter; do not stir.
Spoon pie filling over batter; do not stir.
Bake 40 to 45 minutes or until a toothpick
inserted in center of cobbler crust comes
out clean. Serve warm or transfer to a wire
rack to cool.

Yield: about 8 servings

Chocolate-Cherry Tart (left) *is a sweet, nutty delight that has a chocolate cookie crumb crust. Strawberry-Rhubarb* [*can be enjoyed all year-round with frozen sliced rhubarb and canned strawberry pie filling.*

STRAWBERRY-RHUBARB PIE

- 3/4 cup sugar
- 2 tablespoons cornstarch
- 1/2 teaspoon ground cinnamon
- 1 package (16 ounces) frozen sliced rhubarb, thawed
- 2 cans (21 ounces each) strawberry pie filling
- 2 tablespoons frozen orange juice concentrate
- 1 crust from a 15-ounce package of refrigerated pie crusts, at room temperature
  Egg white, beaten
  Sugar

Preheat oven to 375 degrees. Combine 3/4 cup sugar, cornstarch, and cinnamon in a large bowl. Stir in rhubarb until well coated with sugar mixture; allow to stand 15 minutes. Stir pie filling and juice concentrate into rhubarb mixture. Spoon filling into a 9 x 9 x 2-inch baking dish. On a lightly floured surface, unfold pie crust and use a floured rolling pin to roll out crust to about a 12-inch circle. Using a fluted pastry wheel, cut 3/4-inch-wide strips. Use strips to make lattice top and braided strips around edge of baking dish. Brush crust with egg white and sprinkle with sugar. Bake 50 to 55 minutes or until filling is bubbly and crust is golden brown. Serve warm or transfer to a wire rack to cool.

Yield: 8 to 10 servings

CHOCOLATE-CHERRY TART

FILLING
- 2 cans (14.5 ounces each) tart pitted cherries packed in water
- 1/4 cup cornstarch
- 1 cup sugar
- 1/3 cup chopped toasted slivered almonds
- 1 teaspoon almond extract
- 1/8 teaspoon red liquid food coloring

CRUST
- 1 1/2 cups chocolate wafer cookie crumbs (about 28 cookies)
- 6 tablespoons butter or margarine, melted

  Whipped cream and maraschino cherries to garnish

...or filling, drain cherries, reserving
...up liquid. Combine reserved cherry
...id and cornstarch in a small bowl.
...bine drained cherries and sugar in a
...ium saucepan over medium-high heat.
...ing frequently, cook until sugar
...olves and liquid begins to boil. Stir in
...astarch mixture; reduce heat to
...lium-low. Continue to cook about
...inutes or until mixture thickens.
...ove from heat; stir in almonds, almond
...act, and food coloring. Cover and chill.
...or crust, combine cookie crumbs and
...ted butter in a medium bowl. Press
...ture into bottom and up sides of a lightly
...ased 9-inch-diameter tart pan with a
...ovable bottom. Cover and chill 1 hour
...until firm.
...poon filling into crust. To serve, remove
...es of pan. Garnish tart with whipped
...am and maraschino cherries.

...d: about 10 servings

...EAMY STRAWBERRY PIE

1 package (10 ounces)
      marshmallows
1 package (16 ounces) frozen
      whole strawberries, thawed and
      drained
3 tablespoons strawberry liqueur *or*
      strawberry juice
1 cup whipping cream, whipped
1 purchased large graham cracker
      pie crust (9 ounces)
   Fresh strawberries to garnish

...Place marshmallows in a medium
...crowave-safe bowl. Microwave on high
...ver (100%) 1½ to 2 minutes or until
...rshmallows melt, stirring every
...seconds. Beat in strawberries and
...ueur. Fold in whipped cream. Spoon
...o crust. Cover and chill. Garnish with
...awberries.

...d: about 10 servings

Light and airy, Creamy Strawberry Pie is quick to whip up with frozen fruit, melted marshmallows, and a dash of strawberry liqueur.

CHOCOLATE-BUTTERSCOTCH I

    1 can (5 ounces) evaporated milk
    1 egg yolk
    1 package (6 ounces) semisweet
         chocolate chips
    1 cup butterscotch chips
    1 container (8 ounces) frozen non-
         dairy whipped topping, thawed
    1 purchased vanilla wafer crumb
         pie crust (6 ounces)

       Chopped pecans and chocolate
         sprinkles to garnish

Whisk evaporated milk and egg yolk in
heavy medium saucepan over medium-lo
heat. Whisking constantly, cook 5 to
6 minutes or until mixture becomes hot a
slightly thickened. Reduce heat to low. Ad
chocolate and butterscotch chips; stir un
melted and smooth. Cool to room
temperature; fold in whipped topping.
Spoon into crust. Garnish with pecans an
chocolate sprinkles. Cover and freeze unt
firm enough to slice.

Yield: about 8 servings

WALNUT-FUDGE PIE

    1 cup sugar
  1/2 cup butter or margarine, melted
  1/2 cup all-purpose flour
  1/2 cup chopped walnuts
    2 eggs
  1/4 cup cocoa
    8 walnut halves
  1/4 cup milk chocolate chips
    1 teaspoon shortening

Combine sugar, butter, flour, chopped
walnuts, eggs, and cocoa in a medium bo
beat until well blended. Spread batter into
greased 9-inch microwave-safe pie plate.
Microwave on medium power (60%)
10 to 12 minutes or until almost set in
center (do not overbake). Transfer to a
wire rack. Arrange walnut halves on pie.

Chocolate sprinkles and chopped pecans add richness to Chocolate-Butterscotch Pie, a delightfully simple frozen treat.

Wonderfully chewy and chocolaty, Walnut-Fudge Pie (left) can be baked in minutes in the microwave. Easy Sweet [Po]tato Pie combines old-fashioned goodness with modern convenience — it's made using canned sweet potatoes [an]d a frozen crust.

[Co]mbine chocolate chips and shortening in [a s]mall microwave-safe bowl. Microwave on [hig]h power (100%) 1 minute or until [cho]colate softens; stir until smooth. Spoon [me]lted chocolate mixture into a pastry bag [fitt]ed with a very small tip. Pipe chocolate [on]to warm pie; cool completely.

[Yie]ld: about 8 servings

EASY SWEET POTATO PIE

$^1/_4$ cup butter or margarine, softened
$^2/_3$ cup sugar
1 can (16 ounces) cut sweet
   potatoes in syrup, drained
1 can (5 ounces) evaporated milk
2 eggs
1 teaspoon pumpkin pie spice
1 9-inch unbaked deep-dish pie crust
  Whipped cream and pumpkin pie
   spice to garnish

Preheat oven to 375 degrees. Cream butter and sugar in a medium bowl until fluffy. Add sweet potatoes, evaporated milk, eggs, and pumpkin pie spice. Pour into crust. Bake 40 to 45 minutes or until center is set and crust is lightly browned. Cool on a wire rack. Garnish with whipped cream and pumpkin pie spice. Store in an airtight container in refrigerator.

Yield: about 8 servings

APRICOT CRISP

    2 cans (17 ounces each) apricot
         halves in heavy syrup, drained
         and sliced
    2 tablespoons butter or margarine,
         melted
  1/2 teaspoon ground cinnamon
  1/2 teaspoon almond extract
    1 cup all-purpose flour
  3/4 cup firmly packed brown sugar
  1/4 cup finely chopped pecans
  1/2 cup butter or margarine
       Vanilla ice cream to serve

Preheat oven to 350 degrees. Place
apricot slices in a lightly greased 9-inch
square baking dish. In a small bowl,
combine melted butter, cinnamon, and
almond extract. Pour butter mixture over
apricots. In a medium bowl, combine flour
brown sugar, and pecans. Using a pastry
blender or 2 knives, cut in 1/2 cup butter
until mixture resembles coarse meal.
Sprinkle over apricots. Bake 35 to
40 minutes or until topping is golden
brown. Serve warm with ice cream.

Yield: about 9 servings

BLUEBERRY-LEMON TARTS

    1 can (14 ounces) sweetened
         condensed milk
    1 can (6 ounces) frozen lemonade
         concentrate, thawed
    1 container (8 ounces) frozen non-
         dairy whipped topping, thawed
    4 packages (4 ounces each) of
         6 individual-serving graham
         cracker pie crusts
    1 can (21 ounces) blueberry pie
         filling, chilled
       Lemon zest strips to garnish

In a medium bowl, combine sweetened
condensed milk and lemonade concentra
Fold in whipped topping. Spoon about

*Frozen lemonade concentrate adds tangy sweetness to Blueberry-Lemon
Tarts (left). The creamy pastries are quick to make using little graham cracker
pie crusts. Served warm, Apricot Crisp is a dessert they'll ask for again and
again — and it's a snap to create using canned fruit.*

Hazelnuts baked in the crust offer an unusually delicious flavor to the tropical taste of Banana Cream Tart. Fresh banana slices are layered under the luscious custard filling, which is quick to prepare in the microwave.

...ablespoons lemon mixture into each ...ust. Cover and chill. To serve, top each ...t with 1 heaping tablespoon chilled pie ...ing. Garnish with lemon zest.

...eld: 2 dozen tarts

...ANANA CREAM TART

...RUST

- ³/4 cup toasted hazelnuts
- ¹/2 cup all-purpose flour
- ¹/4 cup butter or margarine, softened
- 2 tablespoons firmly packed brown sugar
- ¹/4 teaspoon salt

...LLING

- ¹/3 cup sugar
- ¹/4 cup all-purpose flour
- ¹/8 teaspoon salt
- 2 eggs
- 1³/4 cups half and half
- ¹/4 cup butter or margarine, cut into pieces
- 3 tablespoons banana-flavored liqueur
- 1 teaspoon vanilla extract
- 2 bananas

   Banana slices and melted white chocolate to garnish

Preheat oven to 350 degrees. For crust, process all ingredients in a food processor until hazelnuts are coarsely ground and ingredients are well blended. Press mixture into bottom and up sides of an ungreased 9-inch-diameter tart pan with a removable bottom. Bake 11 to 13 minutes or until crust is firm. Cool in pan on a wire rack.

For filling, combine sugar, flour, and salt in a small bowl. In a medium microwave-safe bowl, whisk eggs until frothy. Whisk half and half and dry ingredients into eggs. Add butter. Microwave on medium-high power (80%) 3 minutes; whisk mixture. Continue to microwave until mixture is thick enough to coat the back of a spoon, whisking every 3 minutes. Add liqueur and vanilla; whisk until smooth. Place plastic wrap directly on surface of filling; chill 1 hour.

Slice 2 bananas over bottom of crust. Spoon filling over bananas. To serve, remove sides of pan. Garnish tart with banana slices and drizzle with melted white chocolate. Store in an airtight container in refrigerator.

Yield: about 10 servings

17

Using pie crust mix and canned pie filling lets you prepare classic Apple-Cheddar Pie with ease. The crust of this fruit-packed delight is made with sharp Cheddar cheese, and the spiced filling is enriched with pecans and raisins.

APPLE-CHEDDAR PIE

1 package (11 ounces) pie crust mix
1 package (4 ounces) shredded sharp Cheddar cheese, at room temperature
4 to 5 tablespoons cold water
2 cans (21 ounces each) apple pie filling
1/3 cup finely chopped pecans
1/3 cup golden raisins
1/4 cup firmly packed brown sugar
1/2 teaspoon apple pie spice
1/8 teaspoon salt

Preheat oven to 425 degrees. For crust, process pie crust mix, cheese, and water in a food processor until well blended and dough forms a ball. Divide dough in half and shape into 2 balls. Roll out 1 ball of dough between sheets of plastic wrap. Transfer to a 9-inch deep-dish pie plate. Roll out second ball of dough between plastic wrap for top crust. Cut leaf-shaped pieces of dough from center of top crust and reserve.

In a large bowl, combine pie filling, pecans, raisins, brown sugar, apple pie spice, and salt; pour into crust. Place top crust on filling and flute edges. Arrange reserved dough leaves on crust. Bake 40 to 45 minutes or until filling is bubbly and crust is golden brown. If edges of crust brown too quickly, cover with a strip of aluminum foil. Serve warm or transfer to a wire rack to cool.

Yield: 8 to 10 servings

CONUT-PINEAPPLE PIE

- /4 cups sugar
- 4 eggs
- /4 cup butter or margarine, melted
- 1 tablespoon lemon juice
- /8 teaspoon salt
- 1 can (15½ ounces) crushed
      pineapple, drained
- /2 cup finely shredded coconut
- 1 9-inch unbaked deep-dish pie crust

Preheat oven to 350 degrees. In a large
bowl, combine sugar, eggs, melted butter,
lemon juice, and salt; beat until well
blended. Stir in pineapple and coconut;
pour into crust. Bake 45 to 50 minutes or
until center is set. Serve warm or transfer to
wire rack to cool. Store in an airtight
container in refrigerator.

Yield: about 8 servings

PEANUT BUTTER PIE

- 3/4 cup smooth peanut butter
- 2/3 cup dark corn syrup
- 2/3 cup firmly packed brown sugar
- 3 eggs
- 3 tablespoons butter or margarine,
      melted
- 2 teaspoons vanilla extract
- 1/8 teaspoon salt
- 1 9-inch unbaked pie crust
- 1 cup coarsely chopped peanuts

Preheat oven to 400 degrees. Combine
peanut butter, corn syrup, brown sugar,
eggs, melted butter, vanilla, and salt in a
large bowl; beat until well blended. Pour
into crust. Sprinkle peanuts over filling.
Bake 10 minutes. Reduce oven to
350 degrees and bake 35 to 40 minutes
or until center is set. Transfer to a wire
rack to cool. Store in an airtight container
in refrigerator.

Yield: about 8 servings

Coconut-Pineapple Pie (top) *is quick to stir up with a few simple ingredients
you probably have in your cupboard. Peanut lovers will go nuts over Peanut
Butter Pie! Flavored with dark corn syrup and brown sugar, it's packed with
smooth peanut butter.*

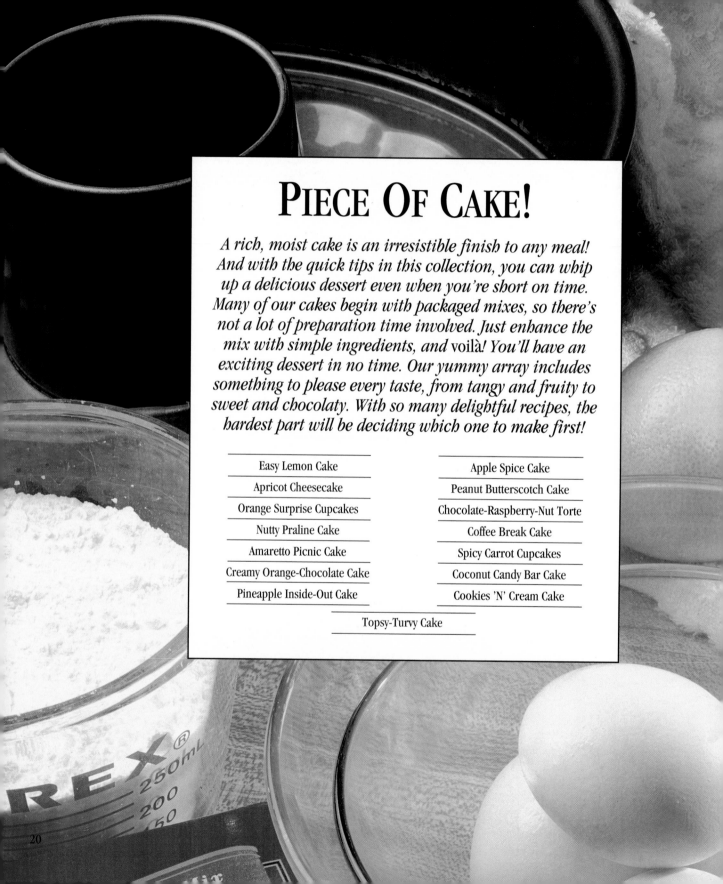

PIECE OF CAKE!

A rich, moist cake is an irresistible finish to any meal! And with the quick tips in this collection, you can whip up a delicious dessert even when you're short on time. Many of our cakes begin with packaged mixes, so there's not a lot of preparation time involved. Just enhance the mix with simple ingredients, and voilà! You'll have an exciting dessert in no time. Our yummy array includes something to please every taste, from tangy and fruity to sweet and chocolaty. With so many delightful recipes, the hardest part will be deciding which one to make first!

Z (1 LB 2.25 OZ) 517g   ADD E

FROZEN CONCENTRATE FOR
LEMONADE

NET 12 FL. OZ. 354 mL   MAKES 64 FL. OZ.   KEE

CONTAINS 15% JUICE

Nutrition Facts
Serv. Size 3 Tablespoons (45mL)*
Servings 8
Calories 110
  Fat Cal. 0
*Makes 8 fl. oz. (240 mL) lemonade

Amount/Serving	%DV**	Amount/S
Total Fat 0g	0%	**Total Ca**
Sat. Fat 0g	0%	Fiber
Cholest. 0mg	0%	Sugar
Sodium 0mg	0%	**Protein**
Vitamin A 0%	:	Vitamin
Calcium 0%	:	Iron 0%

...CTOSE CORN SYRUP, WAT...
...RATE, LEMON PULP.

D-2184

K JIPS-L (PRESERVATIVE), YELLOW 6.
NO— AND DIGLYCERIDES (PREVENT
RNSTARCH MODIFIED, SODIUM, HYDRO-
ING), NATURAL FLAVOR, HYDRO-
(PRESERVATIVE), YELLOW 6.
...L PLAINS, NY 10625, USA

O-L
PUDDING &
PIE FILLING K

For a bold, fruity flavor, try our Easy Lemon Cake. It's quick to whip up using cake mix and instant lemon pudding mix! Topped with a citrusy glaze, this treat will add a little zing to a luncheon or tea party.

EASY LEMON CAKE

- 1 package (18.25 ounces) yellow cake mix
- 4 eggs
- 3/4 cup water
- 3/4 cup vegetable oil
- 1 package (3.4 ounces) lemon instant pudding mix
- 1 cup sifted confectioners sugar
- 1/3 cup frozen lemonade concentrate
- 2 tablespoons butter or margarine
  Lemon slices to decorate

Preheat oven to 350 degrees. In a large bowl, combine cake mix, eggs, water, oil, and pudding mix. Beat at low speed of an electric mixer 30 seconds. Beat at medium speed 2 minutes. Pour batter into a greased 10-inch springform pan with fluted tube insert or a 10-inch fluted tube pan. Bake 40 to 45 minutes or until a toothpick inserted in center of cake comes out clean. Cool in pan 15 minutes; remove sides of pan. Invert cake onto a serving plate. Use a wooden skewer to poke holes about 1 inch apart in top of warm cake. Combine confectioners sugar, lemonade concentrate, and butter in a heavy small saucepan over medium-high heat. Bring to a boil; remove from heat. Slowly pour glaze over warm cake; cool completely. Place lemon slices around bottom of cake to decorate.

Yield: about 16 servings

APRICOT CHEESECAKE

CRUST

- 6 tablespoons butter or margarine
- 1/4 cup sugar
- 1 cup vanilla wafer crumbs (about 30 cookies)

FILLING

- 1 can (17 ounces) apricot halves, divided
- 1 package (3 ounces) apricot gelatin
- 2 packages (8 ounces each) cream cheese, softened
- 1 can (14 ounces) sweetened condensed milk
- 2 tablespoons orange juice
  Fresh mint leaves to garnish

or crust, combine butter and sugar in a
[me]dium saucepan over medium-high heat.
[Stir]ring constantly, bring to a boil; remove
[from] heat. Stir in vanilla wafer crumbs.
[Pre]ss crumb mixture into bottom of an
[g]reased 9-inch springform pan; chill.
[F]or filling, drain apricots, reserving
[⅓] cup juice. Combine reserved apricot
[juic]e and gelatin in a small saucepan over
[me]dium heat. Stir frequently until gelatin
[dis]solves; remove from heat.
[I]n a large bowl, beat cream cheese until
[fluf]fy. Reserving 2 apricot halves for
[gar]nish, add remaining apricots, gelatin
[mix]ture, sweetened condensed milk, and
[ora]nge juice; beat with an electric mixer
[unti]l well blended. Pour over crust. Cover
[and] chill 4 hours or until firm.
[T]o serve, remove sides of pan. Garnish
[with] reserved apricot halves and mint
[lea]ves. Store in an airtight container in
[refr]igerator.

[Yie]ld: about 16 servings

[O]RANGE SURPRISE CUPCAKES

2   packages (3 ounces each) cream
    cheese, softened
[¼]   cup sugar
1   egg white
[⅓]   cup semisweet chocolate mini
    chips
1   package (18.25 ounces) orange
    cake mix
[1]⅓   cups water
3   eggs
[⅓]   cup vegetable oil

Preheat oven to 350 degrees. In a
[me]dium bowl, beat cream cheese, sugar,
[an]d egg white until fluffy. Stir in chocolate
[ch]ips. In a large bowl, combine cake mix,
[wa]ter, eggs, and oil. Beat at low speed of an
[ele]ctric mixer 30 seconds. Beat at medium
[sp]eed 2 minutes. Spoon batter into paper-
[lin]ed muffin cups, filling each about two-

Smooth and creamy are the best words to describe our Apricot Cheesecake (right). Sweetened condensed milk makes it easy to create the rich, fruity dessert. Prepared with cake mix and a few other ingredients, moist Orange Surprise Cupcakes have a secret hidden in the middle — a filling of cream cheese and chocolate chips!

thirds full. Drop a tablespoonful of cream cheese mixture into center of batter in each muffin cup. Bake 18 to 21 minutes or until cake springs back when lightly touched. Transfer cupcakes to a wire rack to cool. Store in an airtight container in refrigerator.

Yield: about 2 dozen cupcakes

NUTTY PRALINE CAKE

CAKE

> 1 cup firmly packed brown sugar
> 1/2 cup butter or margarine
> 1/4 cup whipping cream
> 3/4 cup chopped pecans
> 1/2 teaspoon vanilla extract
> 1 package (18.25 ounces) caramel cake mix
> 1 1/3 cups water
> 3 eggs
> 1/3 cup vegetable oil

ICING

> 1 package (3 ounces) cream cheese softened
> 1/4 cup plus 2 teaspoons milk
> 4 cups sifted confectioners sugar
> 1/2 cup butterscotch chips, melted

Preheat oven to 325 degrees. For cake combine brown sugar, butter, and whipp cream in a heavy small saucepan. Stirring constantly, cook over medium-low heat until butter melts and mixture is well blended. Stir in pecans and vanilla. Pour mixture into 2 greased 9-inch round cake pans. In a large bowl, combine cake mix, water, eggs, and oil. Beat at low speed of electric mixer 30 seconds. Beat at medium speed 2 minutes. Slowly pour batter over pecan mixture. Bake 30 to 35 minutes or until a toothpick inserted in center of cake comes out clean. Cool in pans 5 minutes. Invert onto a wire rack with waxed paper underneath; cool completely.

For icing, beat cream cheese and milk a medium bowl until well blended. Gradually add confectioners sugar, continuing to beat until smooth. Add melt butterscotch chips; beat until well blended. With praline layers up, spread icing betwe layers and on top of cake. Store in an airtight container in refrigerator.

Yield: 12 to 14 servings

Featuring the flavor of a delectable candy, this Nutty Praline Cake is unforgettable! The super-moist cake, made with a packaged mix, is layered with a praline mixture and topped with cream cheese-butterscotch icing.

...ARETTO PICNIC CAKE

- ...1 cup finely chopped toasted almonds
- ...1 package (27.25 ounces) cake mix with streusel topping and glaze mix
- ...1 cup brewed amaretto-flavored coffee
- ...3 eggs
- ...1/4 cup plus 2 tablespoons amaretto, divided
- ...1/3 cup vegetable oil
- ...1 tablespoon amaretto-flavored non-dairy powdered creamer

...reheat oven to 350 degrees. In a small ...wl, combine almonds and package of ...usel topping. In a large bowl, combine ...e mix, coffee, eggs, 1/4 cup amaretto, oil, ...creamer. Beat at low speed of an ...ctric mixer 30 seconds. Beat at medium ...ed 2 minutes. Sprinkle half of streusel ...ping mixture into bottom of a greased ...inch fluted tube pan. Spoon two-thirds of ...er over streusel topping. Repeat layers ...g remaining topping and batter. Bake ...to 45 minutes or until a toothpick ...erted in center of cake comes out clean. ...l in pan 10 minutes. Invert onto a ...ving plate; cool completely.

...ombine package of glaze mix and ...aining 2 tablespoons amaretto; drizzle ...r cake.

...d: about 16 servings

...REAMY ORANGE-CHOCOLATE ...KE

- ...1 package (18.25 ounces) chocolate fudge cake mix with pudding in the mix
- ...1 cup water
- ...3 eggs
- ...1/3 cup vegetable oil
- ...1/3 cup plus 1 tablespoon orange-flavored liqueur, divided

A soothing blend of amaretto and flavored coffee and creamer lend wonderful taste to our Amaretto Picnic Cake (top). Creamy Orange-Chocolate Cake is a spirited treat made with fudge cake mix and orange liqueur. For a finishing touch, ready-to-spread frosting is enhanced with orange marmalade.

- 1 container (16 ounces) chocolate fudge ready-to-spread frosting
- 1/4 cup orange marmalade
  Orange slice and fresh mint leaves to garnish

Preheat oven to 350 degrees. In a large bowl, combine cake mix, water, eggs, oil, and 1/3 cup liqueur. Beat at low speed of an electric mixer 30 seconds. Beat at medium speed 2 minutes. Pour batter into 3 greased 9-inch round cake pans. Bake 20 to 25 minutes or until a toothpick inserted in center of cake comes out clean. Cool in pans 15 minutes. Remove from pans and cool completely on a wire rack.

Combine frosting, orange marmalade, and remaining 1 tablespoon liqueur in a medium bowl; stir until well blended. Spread glaze between layers and on top of cake. Garnish with orange slice and mint leaves.

Yield: 12 to 14 servings

Crowned with cherries, pineapple, and a sweet glaze, our Pineapple Inside-Out Cake is made with cake mix and crushed pineapple. With just one mouth-watering bite, it's destined to become a favorite!

PINEAPPLE INSIDE-OUT CAKE

1 package (18.25 ounces)
  pineapple cake mix
1 can (15½ ounces) crushed
  pineapple in heavy syrup,
  divided
4 eggs
½ cup vegetable oil
¼ cup granulated sugar
1 cup sifted confectioners sugar
  Chopped maraschino cherries
  to garnish

Preheat oven to 350 degrees. In a large bowl, combine cake mix, 1 cup undrained pineapple, eggs, oil, and granulated sugar. Beat at low speed of an electric mixer 30 seconds. Beat at medium speed 2 minutes. Pour into a greased 10-inch fluted tube pan. Bake 50 to 55 minutes or until a toothpick inserted in center of cake comes out clean. Cool in pan 15 minutes. Invert onto serving plate; cool completely.

Drain remaining pineapple, reserving pineapple juice. Combine confectioners sugar and 5 teaspoons reserved pineapple juice in a small bowl; stir until smooth. Drizzle glaze over cake. Garnish with reserved drained pineapple and cherries.

Yield: about 16 servings

APPLE SPICE CAKE

CAKE

1 package (18.25 ounces) spice
  cake mix
1 cup apple juice
3 eggs
⅓ cup applesauce
⅓ cup vegetable oil
1 teaspoon maple flavoring
2 cups cored, unpeeled, and
  chopped Granny Smith apples
  (about 2 apples)

TOPPING

½ cup applesauce
⅓ cup firmly packed brown sugar
¼ cup butter or margarine

Preheat oven to 325 degrees. For cake, combine cake mix, apple juice, eggs, applesauce, oil, and maple flavoring in a large bowl. Beat at low speed of an electric mixer 30 seconds. Beat at medium speed 2 minutes. Stir in apples. Pour batter into a greased 9 x 13-inch baking dish. Bake 40 to 45 minutes or until a toothpick inserted in center of cake comes out clean. Place baking dish on a wire rack while making topping.

For topping, combine all ingredients in a small saucepan over medium-high heat. Stirring frequently, bring to a boil; reduce heat and cook until thickened. Serve warm cake with topping.

Yield: about 16 servings

PEANUT BUTTERSCOTCH CAKE

1/3 cup smooth peanut butter
1   package (18.25 ounces) white
       cake mix
1   package (3.5 ounces)
       butterscotch pudding mix
1   cup water
4   eggs
1/4 cup vegetable oil

Preheat oven to 350 degrees. Stirring frequently, melt peanut butter in a small saucepan over medium heat. Remove from heat. In a large bowl, combine cake mix, pudding mix, water, eggs, and oil. Beat at low speed of an electric mixer 30 seconds. Beat at medium speed 2 minutes. Add 2 cups batter to peanut butter. Pour remaining batter into a greased 10-inch tube pan. Spoon peanut butter mixture over batter. Bake 50 to 55 minutes or until a toothpick inserted in center of cake comes out clean. Cool in pan 15 minutes. Remove from pan and cool completely on a wire rack.

Yield: about 16 servings

For a rich delight, try our Apple Spice Cake (right). Made with applesauce and spice cake mix and served with an applesauce topping, it's sure to please. A delightful taste sensation awaits in our Peanut Butterscotch Cake. It's flavored with peanut butter and butterscotch pudding mix for a deliciously different dessert.

This Chocolate-Raspberry-Nut Torte looks so elegant, no one will believe how simple it is to prepare using chocolate fudge cake mix. Melted raspberry jam, rich chocolate pudding, and whipped topping provide the finishing touches.

CHOCOLATE-RASPBERRY-NUT TORTE

1 package (18.25 ounces)
   chocolate fudge cake mix with
   pudding in the mix
1¹/₃ cups water
3 eggs
¹/₃ cup vegetable oil
1 cup coarsely ground toasted
   pecans, divided
1 package (3.9 ounces) chocolate
   fudge instant pudding mix
1³/₄ cups milk
¹/₂ cup seedless raspberry jam
1 container (4 ounces) frozen
   non-dairy whipped topping,
   thawed
   Frozen or fresh whole red
   raspberries to garnish

Preheat oven to 350 degrees. Grease three 9-inch round cake pans and line bottoms with waxed paper. In a large bowl, combine cake mix, water, eggs, and oil. Beat at low speed of an electric mixer 30 seconds. Beat at medium speed 2 minutes. Stir in ³/₄ cup pecans. Pour batter into prepared pans. Bake 15 to 20 minutes or until a toothpick inserted in center of cake comes out clean. Cool in pans 10 minutes. Remove from pans and cool completely on a wire rack.

In a medium bowl, add pudding mix to milk; beat until thickened. Cover and chill 10 minutes.

Stirring frequently, melt jam in a small saucepan over medium heat. Brush melted jam over each cake layer. Place 1 layer on serving plate. Spread about 1 cup pudding over layer. Repeat with second layer and remaining pudding. Top with third layer. Spread whipped topping on top of cake. serve, garnish with remaining ¹/₄ cup pecans and raspberries. Store in an airtig container in refrigerator.

Yield: 12 to 14 servings

COFFEE BREAK CAKE

1 cup crushed chocolate-covered
   graham crackers
1 cup chopped pecans
2 teaspoons ground cinnamon
1 package (18.25 ounces) yellow
   cake mix

¼ cups water
3 eggs
⅓ cup vegetable oil
½ cup sifted confectioners sugar
2 teaspoons milk
1 teaspoon vanilla extract

Preheat oven to 350 degrees. In a small
bowl, combine cracker crumbs, pecans,
and cinnamon. In a large bowl, combine
cake mix, water, eggs, and oil. Beat at low
speed of an electric mixer 30 seconds. Beat
at medium speed 2 minutes. Pour batter
into a greased 10-inch tube pan. Sprinkle
cracker crumb mixture over batter. Bake
30 to 40 minutes or until a toothpick
inserted in center of cake comes out clean.
Cool in pan 15 minutes. Remove from pan
and cool completely on a wire rack.

In a small bowl, combine confectioners
sugar, milk, and vanilla; stir until smooth.
Drizzle glaze over cake.

Yield: about 16 servings

SPICY CARROT CUPCAKES

1 package (18.25 ounces) spice
      cake mix
1⅓ cups water
3 eggs
⅓ cup vegetable oil
1¼ cups finely shredded carrots
      (about 4 carrots)
¾ cup finely chopped toasted
      walnuts, divided
1 cup flaked coconut, toasted and
      divided
2 packages (3 ounces each) cream
      cheese, softened
⅓ cup butter or margarine, softened
3 tablespoons sifted confectioners
      sugar
1½ tablespoons maple syrup

Preheat oven to 350 degrees. In a large
bowl, combine cake mix, water, eggs, and

Our Coffee Break Cake (left) *is a delicious reason to stop and have a snack
— and it's ready in a jiffy! It features a cinnamony streusel topping made with
crushed chocolate-covered graham crackers. Ordinary spice cake mix is
combined with carrots, walnuts, and coconut to create Spicy Carrot Cupcakes.
The tasty treats are topped with a maple-flavored cream cheese icing.*

oil. Beat at low speed of an electric mixer
30 seconds. Beat at medium speed
2 minutes. Stir in carrots, ½ cup walnuts,
and ½ cup coconut. Fill paper-lined muffin
cups about three-fourths full. Bake 15 to
20 minutes or until a toothpick inserted in
center of cupcake comes out clean.
Transfer cupcakes to a wire rack to cool.

In a small bowl, beat cream cheese and
butter until fluffy. Add confectioners sugar
and maple syrup; continue to beat until
smooth. Ice cupcakes. Sprinkle remaining
¼ cup walnuts and ½ cup coconut over
icing. Store in an airtight container in
refrigerator.

Yield: about 2½ dozen cupcakes

29

Rich devil's food cake, prepared from a mix, becomes sinfully delicious when layered with a sweet marshmallow-coconut filling. Ready-to-spread fudge frosting finishes our stunning Coconut Candy Bar Cake.

COCONUT CANDY BAR CAKE

- 1 cup sugar
- 1 cup evaporated milk
- 1/2 cup butter or margarine
- 24 marshmallows
- 1 package (14 ounces) flaked coconut
- 2 9-inch-round devil's food cake layers (prepared from a cake mix)
- 1 container (16 ounces) chocolate fudge ready-to-spread frosting

In a medium saucepan, combine sugar, evaporated milk, and butter over medium-high heat. Stirring frequently, bring mixture to a boil. Reduce heat to medium; continue to stir and cook 2 minutes. Remove from heat. Stir in marshmallows until melted. Stir in coconut. Chill filling 1 hour.

Cut each cake layer in half to make 4 thin layers. Spread filling evenly between layers. Spread frosting on top and sides of cake. Store in an airtight container in refrigerator.

Yield: 12 to 14 servings

COOKIES 'N' CREAM CAKE

- 1 package (18.25 ounces) white cake mix
- 1 1/4 cups water
- 1/3 cup vegetable oil
- 3 egg whites
- 1 1/2 cups coarsely crushed chocolate sandwich cookies (about 14 cookies), divided
- 1 package (3 ounces) cream cheese softened
- 2 tablespoons butter or margarine, softened

3 cups sifted confectioners sugar

2 teaspoon vanilla extract

2 to 3 tablespoons milk

Chocolate sandwich cookie halves
to decorate

reheat oven to 350 degrees. In a large
l, combine cake mix, water, oil, and egg
es. Beat at low speed of an electric
er 30 seconds. Beat at medium speed
inutes. Stir in 1 cup crushed cookies by
d. Pour batter into 2 greased and
red 9-inch round cake pans. Bake 20 to
ninutes or until a toothpick inserted in
ter of cake comes out clean. Cool in
s 15 minutes. Remove from pans and
completely on a wire rack.
n a medium bowl, beat cream cheese
butter until fluffy. Stir in confectioners
ar, vanilla, and enough milk for desired
ading consistency; beat until smooth.
e 1 cake layer, top side down, on
ing plate; spread about one-fourth of
g over layer. Top with remaining cake
r. Spread remaining icing on top and
s of cake. Sprinkle remaining ¹/₂ cup
shed cookies on top of cake. Place
kie halves around bottom of cake to
orate. Store in an airtight container in
igerator.

d: 12 to 14 servings

PSY-TURVY CAKE

1 cup chopped pecans

1 cup flaked coconut

2 packages (3 ounces each) cream
cheese, softened

¹/₃ cup butter or margarine, softened

1 ounce semisweet baking
chocolate, melted

1 teaspoon vanilla extract

1 package (16 ounces)
confectioners sugar

1 package (18.25 ounces) devil's
food cake mix with pudding in
the mix

*Plain white cake is given a new twist in our Cookies 'N' Cream Cake (left).
Simply add crushed chocolate sandwich cookies to a purchased cake mix and
top with rich cream cheese icing. A gooey chocolate indulgence, Topsy-Turvy
Cake makes its own topping as it bakes! The tasty delight is made with devil's
food cake mix, cream cheese, coconut, and pecans.*

1¹/₄ cups water

3 eggs

¹/₃ cup vegetable oil

Preheat oven to 350 degrees. Combine
pecans and coconut in a greased
9 x 13-inch baking pan. In a medium bowl,
beat cream cheese and butter until fluffy;
beat in melted chocolate and vanilla. Add
confectioners sugar; beat until well blended.
In a large bowl, combine cake mix, water,
eggs, and oil. Beat at low speed of an
electric mixer 30 seconds. Beat at medium
speed 2 minutes. Pour batter over pecan
mixture. Drop tablespoonfuls of cream
cheese mixture over cake batter to within
1 inch of edges. Bake 50 minutes or until
cake pulls away from sides of pan. Cool in
pan 15 minutes. Serve warm. Store in an
airtight container in refrigerator.

Yield: about 16 servings

SO-QUICK SWEETS

Generations of homemakers have found that nothing says "I love you" like a tray of homemade cookies or candies. And a moist, delicious brownie served with a glass of milk has long been a favorite after-school snack. Our grandmothers spent hours creating these confections, but today's busy women can enjoy time-saving advantages like store-bought mixes, microwave ovens, and creative shortcuts! The recipes in this collection have all the goodness of your childhood treats, but they can be made in just a short time.

CHOCOLATE-HAZELNUT SANDWICH COOKIES

1 package (9½ ounces) brown-edge wafer cookies
1 jar (6.5 ounces) chocolate-hazelnut spread
⅓ cup semisweet chocolate chips

Place half of cookies bottom side up on waxed paper. Place 1 teaspoon hazelnut spread in center of each cookie. Top with remaining cookies; gently press together. Transfer cookies to a wire rack with waxed paper underneath.

In a small microwave-safe bowl, microwave chocolate chips on high power (100%) 1 minute or until chocolate softens; stir until smooth. Spoon into a resealable plastic bag. Snip off 1 corner of bag. Drizzle chocolate over cookies.

Yield: about 2 dozen sandwich cookies

CAPPUCCINO BROWNIES

1 teaspoon instant espresso powder
2 tablespoons warm water
1 package (10.25 ounces) brownie mix
1 egg
3 tablespoons vegetable oil
½ teaspoon ground cinnamon

Preheat oven to 350 degrees. In a medium bowl, combine espresso powder and warm water. Add remaining ingredients; stir until well blended. Spread batter into a greased 8-inch square baking pan. Bake 18 to 22 minutes. Cool in pan on a wire rack. Cut into 1½ x 2-inch bars.

Yield: about 1½ dozen brownies

When unexpected guests arrive, don't panic — Chocolate-Hazelnut Sandwich Cookies can be ready in minutes! Just spread purchased wafers with chocolate-hazelnut spread and drizzle with melted chocolate.

Instant espresso and ground cinnamon add pizzazz to Cappuccino Brownies (lower right), *chocolaty treats made ng packaged brownie mix. Honey-Granola Cookies are simply sugar cookies sweetened with a touch of honey and riched with crunchy granola cereal.*

ONEY-GRANOLA COOKIES

1 package (22.3 ounces) sugar
   cookie mix
2 eggs
/3 cup vegetable oil
2 tablespoons honey
1 teaspoon water
2 cups granola cereal with nuts

Preheat oven to 375 degrees. Place cookie mix in a large bowl; break up lumps with a fork. Stir in eggs, oil, honey, and water until moistened. Stir in cereal. Drop teaspoonfuls of dough 2 inches apart onto an ungreased baking sheet. Bake 7 to

9 minutes or until edges are lightly browned. Transfer cookies to a wire rack to cool.

Yield: about 5 dozen cookies

Microwave Raspberry-Pecan Fudge is delightfully delicious! A dash of raspberry liqueur adds fruity flavor to the creamy confection, which combines semisweet chocolate, evaporated milk, and other goodies.

MICROWAVE RASPBERRY-PECAN FUDGE

- ½ cup butter or margarine
- 1½ cups sugar
- 1 can (5 ounces) evaporated milk
- 2 cups miniature marshmallows
- 1 package (6 ounces) semisweet chocolate chips
- ¾ cup chopped pecans
- 2 tablespoons raspberry-flavored liqueur

Line an 8-inch square baking pan with aluminum foil, extending foil over 2 sides of pan; grease foil. In a large microwave-safe bowl, microwave butter on high power (100%) 1 minute. Stir in sugar and evaporated milk. Microwave on high power 8 minutes, stirring every 2 minutes. Stir in marshmallows and chocolate chips. Microwave on medium-high power (80%) 1 minute; stir until mixture is smooth. Stir in pecans and liqueur. Pour mixture into prepared pan; chill. Use ends of foil to lift fudge from pan. Cut into 1-inch squares. Store in an airtight container in refrigerator.

Yield: about 3½ dozen pieces fudge

RUM-RAISIN BARS

- 1½ cups raisins
- 1½ cups golden raisins
- ⅓ cup rum
- ¼ cup water
- ½ cup butter or margarine, softened
- ⅓ cup firmly packed brown sugar
- 1 cup all-purpose flour
- 1 cup flaked coconut
- 1 cup chopped walnuts
- 1 can (14 ounces) sweetened condensed milk

ombine raisins, rum, and water in a
y small saucepan. Place over medium-
heat and bring to a boil. Remove from
; cover and allow to stand while
aring crust.

reheat oven to 350 degrees. Cream
er and brown sugar in a medium bowl
fluffy. Stir in flour until well blended.
s mixture into bottom of a greased
13-inch baking pan. Bake 10 minutes.
coconut and walnuts into raisin
ture; spread over crust. Pour sweetened
densed milk over mixture. Bake
ninutes or until topping is golden
wn. Cool in pan 15 minutes. Cut into
-inch squares while warm. Cool
pletely in pan.

d: about 4 dozen bars

OCOLATE SHORTBREAD BARS

    cup butter, softened
'3 cup sifted confectioners sugar
4 cup firmly packed brown sugar
4 cups all-purpose flour
4 cup cocoa

reheat oven to 325 degrees. In a large
l, cream butter and sugars until fluffy.
small bowl, combine flour and cocoa.
dually add dry ingredients to creamed
ture; stir just until blended (do not
rmix). Press into bottom of a lightly
ased 9 x 13-inch baking pan. Prick
gh with a fork. Bake 23 to 25 minutes
ntil edges are lightly browned. Cool in
 on a wire rack 10 minutes. Cut warm
tbread into 1 x 2-inch bars. Cool
pletely in pan.

d: about 4 dozen bars

Moist and chewy, Rum-Raisin Bars (top right) *are bursting with plump, juicy raisins and flaked coconut. Created with simple ingredients, Chocolate Shortbread Bars are a natural when you have a craving for chocolate. They're great for dunking in milk!*

HONEY-NUT FUDGE

- ¹/₄ cup butter or margarine
- 3 ounces unsweetened baking chocolate
- ¹/₂ cup honey
- 1 tablespoon water
- 1 teaspoon vanilla extract
- 1 package (16 ounces) confectioners sugar
- 1 cup chopped pecans

Line an 8-inch square baking pan with aluminum foil, extending foil over 2 sides pan; grease foil. In a heavy large saucepa melt butter and chocolate over medium-h heat. Add honey, water, and vanilla to chocolate mixture; stir until well blended Remove from heat. Add confectioners su stir until smooth. Stir in pecans. Spread mixture into prepared pan. Chill until fir Use ends of foil to lift fudge from pan. Cu into 1-inch squares. Store in an airtight container in a cool place.

Yield: about 4 dozen pieces fudge

CRUNCHY PEANUT BUTTER BITES

- 1 cup crunchy peanut butter
- 1 cup sugar
- 1 egg
- 1 teaspoon vanilla extract

Preheat oven to 350 degrees. Combine ingredients in a medium bowl; beat until well blended. Drop teaspoonfuls of doug 2 inches apart onto an ungreased baking sheet. Bake 8 to 10 minutes or until bottoms are lightly browned. Cool cookie on pan 3 minutes; transfer to a wire rack cool completely.

Yield: about 3 dozen cookies

Connoisseurs of fudge will love Honey-Nut Fudge (right), *a sweet treat that gets its unique flavor from pecans and honey. Crunchy Peanut Butter Bites are made with four simple ingredients you probably have on hand.*

A great alternative to pumpkin pie, Orange-Pecan Pumpkin Bars offer the rich flavor of pumpkin and a tantalizing *ture. The buttery delights are quick to make using purchased yellow cake mix, canned pumpkin, cream cheese, and *nge marmalade.

*RANGE-PECAN PUMPKIN BARS

1 package (18.25 ounces) yellow
    cake mix
/4 cup butter or margarine, melted
/2 cup finely chopped pecans
/4 cup orange marmalade, melted
2 packages (3 ounces each) cream
    cheese, softened
1 cup canned pumpkin
/4 cup firmly packed brown sugar
1 egg

1 teaspoon vanilla extract
1/8 teaspoon salt

Preheat oven to 350 degrees. In a medium bowl, combine cake mix and melted butter (mixture will be crumbly). Stir in pecans. Reserve 1 cup cake mix mixture for topping. Press remaining mixture into bottom of a greased 9 x 13-inch baking pan. Spread marmalade over crust. In a medium bowl, beat cream

cheese until fluffy. Add remaining ingredients; beat until smooth. Spread filling over marmalade layer. Sprinkle reserved cake mix mixture over filling. Bake 40 to 45 minutes or until top is lightly browned and filling is set. Cool in pan on a wire rack. Cut into 1 x 2-inch bars. Store in an airtight container in refrigerator.

Yield: about 4 dozen bars

German Chocolate Squares are brownie-like treats that are sure to please! Topped with flaked coconut, the chocolaty dessert can be made in no time using packaged cake mix.

GERMAN CHOCOLATE SQUARES

1 package (18.25 ounces) German chocolate cake mix with pudding in the mix
1/3 cup vegetable oil
1 egg
1 cup sugar
4 eggs
1/2 teaspoon salt
1 cup light corn syrup
1/4 cup butter or margarine, melted
1 teaspoon vanilla extract
2 cups chopped pecans
1 1/2 cups flaked coconut

Preheat oven to 350 degrees. Combine cake mix, oil, and 1 egg in a medium bowl; stir until well blended. Press mixture into bottom of a greased 9 x 13-inch baking dish. Bake 20 minutes. In a large bowl, beat sugar, 4 eggs, and salt until well blended. Beat in corn syrup, melted butter, and vanilla. Stir in pecans and coconut. Pour filling over hot crust. Bake 30 to 35 minut** or until top is lightly browned and center set. Cool in pan on a wire rack. Cut into 1 1/2-inch squares.

Yield: about 3 dozen squares

CHERRY-TOPPED CHOCOLATE COOKIES

1 jar (10 ounces) maraschino
    cherry halves
1 package (18.25 ounces) devil's
    food cake mix
1/2 cup sour cream
1 egg
2 tablespoons confectioners sugar

Preheat oven to 375 degrees. Drain
cherries; place on a paper towel and pat
dry. In a large bowl, beat cake mix, sour
cream, and egg with an electric mixer until
light in color (batter will be stiff). Use
greased hands to shape dough into 1-inch
balls and place 2 inches apart on a greased
baking sheet. Press 1 cherry half into center
of each cookie. Bake 8 to 10 minutes or
until edges are set. Cool cookies on pan
5 minutes; transfer to a wire rack to cool
completely. Sift confectioners sugar over
cookies.

Yield: about 5 dozen cookies

LEMON GLACIER CANDY

2 packages (10¼ ounces each)
    hard lemon drop candies,
    crushed
8 ounces vanilla candy coating

Preheat oven to 300 degrees. Spread
candies on a lightly greased jellyroll pan.
Bake 12 to 14 minutes or until candies
melt, tilting pan as necessary to evenly cover
pan. Place pan on a wire rack to cool.
Stirring frequently, melt candy coating in a
heavy medium saucepan over low heat.
Spread candy coating over candy layer. Chill
30 minutes or until coating hardens. Break
into pieces.

Yield: about 1½ pounds candy

Sprinkled with confectioners sugar, Cherry-Topped Chocolate Cookies (left)
are moist, chewy treats that are made using cake mix and sour cream. Lemon
Glacier Candy is covered with melted vanilla candy coating.

CREAMY LEMON-PECAN CANDIES

1³/₄ cups sugar
1 cup whipping cream
1 cup miniature marshmallows
1 teaspoon dried lemon peel
¹/₂ teaspoon lemon extract
1³/₄ cups chopped pecans

In a large microwave-safe bowl, combine sugar and whipping cream. Microwave on high power (100%) 8 to 12 minutes or until mixture reaches soft-ball stage (approximately 234 to 240 degrees). Test about ¹/₂ teaspoon mixture in ice water. Mixture will easily form a ball in ice water, but will flatten when held in your hand. Without scraping sides, pour candy into another large heat-resistant bowl. Add marshmallows, lemon peel, and lemon extract; beat 3 to 5 minutes or until mixture thickens and begins to lose its gloss. Stir in pecans. Quickly drop teaspoonfuls of candy onto greased waxed paper; cool completely.

Yield: about 3¹/₂ dozen pieces candy

PEANUT BUTTER BARS

1 package (16 ounces)
      confectioners sugar
1¹/₂ cups graham cracker crumbs
1 cup smooth peanut butter
1 cup butter or margarine
8 chocolate-covered caramel,
      peanut, and nougat candy bars,
      chopped (2.07 ounces each)
1 tablespoon milk

Combine confectioners sugar and graham cracker crumbs in a large bowl. In a medium microwave-safe bowl, combine peanut butter and butter. Microwave on medium-high power (80%) 2 minutes or until mixture melts, stirring after each minute. Pour peanut butter mixture over graham cracker mixture; stir until well blended. Press mixture into bottom of an

Creamy Lemon-Pecan Candies (bottom) *and Peanut Butter Bars are quick to make in the microwave. The lemony candies are made with melted marshmallows and chopped pecans, and the buttery bars feature a peanut butter-graham cracker crust topped with a melted candy bar mixture.*

Chocolaty sandwich cookies are hidden inside the wintry cloaks of our Snowball Cookies! The purchased cookies are ~~*ped*~~ *in melted candy coating and rolled in coconut.*

~~g~~reased 9 x 13-inch baking dish. Place ~~an~~dy bar pieces and milk in a medium ~~mi~~crowave-safe bowl. Microwave on ~~me~~dium power (50%) 3 minutes or until ~~can~~dy melts, stirring after each minute. ~~Spr~~ead melted candy mixture over peanut ~~but~~ter mixture. Cool 20 minutes or until ~~can~~dy mixture hardens. Cut into 1-inch ~~squ~~ares.

~~Yie~~ld: about 8 dozen bars

SNOWBALL COOKIES

   3 cups finely shredded coconut
   1 package (18 ounces) vanilla
      candy coating
   1 package (16 ounces) chocolate
      sandwich cookies

Spread coconut on waxed paper. Melt candy coating in a heavy medium saucepan over low heat. Remove from heat. Place each cookie on a fork and dip into candy coating until covered; roll in coconut. Place cookies on waxed paper and allow candy coating to harden.

Yield: about 3$\frac{1}{2}$ dozen cookies

Butter-flavored crackers are sandwiched with a mixture of peanut butter and honey for Honey-Peanut Butter Dips. The cookies are coated with chocolate for a taste your family will never tire of!

HONEY-PEANUT BUTTER DIPS

²/₃ cup smooth peanut butter
3 tablespoons honey
1 package (12 ounces) butter-flavored crackers
22 ounces chocolate candy coating

In a small bowl, combine peanut butter and honey. Place half of crackers on waxed paper. Spoon peanut butter mixture into a pastry bag fitted with a large round tip. Pipe about 1 teaspoon peanut butter mixture onto each cracker. Top with remaining crackers; gently press together. In a heavy medium saucepan, melt candy coating over low heat. Remove from heat. Place each cookie on a fork and dip into candy coating until covered. Place on waxed paper and allow candy coating to harden.

Yield: about 4 dozen sandwich cookies

CHOCOLATE CHIP BARS

1 package (7 ounces) bran muffin
    mix
1/2 cup butter or margarine, melted
1/4 cup firmly packed brown sugar
2 eggs
1 cup semisweet chocolate mini
    chips
1 cup chopped pecans

Preheat oven to 325 degrees. Combine
muffin mix, melted butter, brown sugar, and
eggs in a medium bowl; stir until well
blended. Stir in chocolate chips and pecans.
Spread mixture into a greased 7 x 11-inch
baking pan. Bake 25 to 30 minutes or until
lightly browned. Cool in pan on a wire rack.
Cut into 1 x 2-inch bars.

Yield: about 2½ dozen bars

CHOCOLATE-PEANUT BUTTER
PUFFS

1 package (6 ounces) semisweet
    chocolate chips
1 cup peanut butter chips
1/2 cup coarsely chopped peanuts
30 marshmallows

In a medium microwave-safe bowl,
combine chocolate and peanut butter chips.
Microwave on medium-high power (80%)
2 minutes or until mixture softens; stir until
smooth. Stir in peanuts. Drop about
3 marshmallows at a time into chocolate
mixture; stir to completely cover
marshmallows. Place coated marshmallows
on a baking sheet covered with waxed
paper. Chill until chocolate hardens.

Yield: 2½ dozen pieces candy

*Bran muffin mix adds body to Chocolate Chip Bars (top), flavorful snacks
that are loaded with pecans. Marshmallows are coated with melted chocolate
and peanut butter chips and chopped peanuts to create microwavable
Chocolate-Peanut Butter Puffs.*

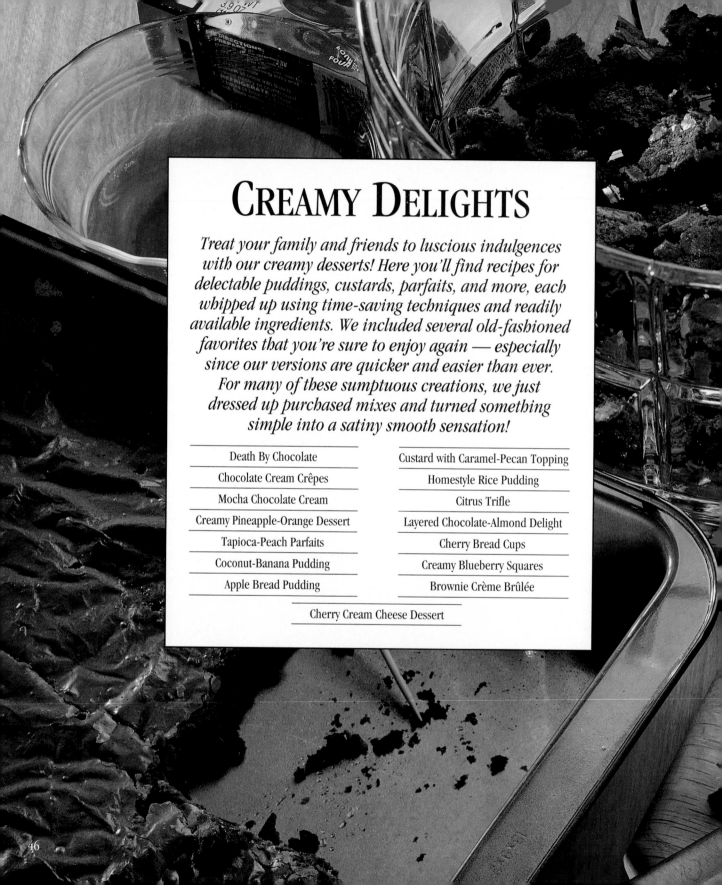

CREAMY DELIGHTS

Treat your family and friends to luscious indulgences with our creamy desserts! Here you'll find recipes for delectable puddings, custards, parfaits, and more, each whipped up using time-saving techniques and readily available ingredients. We included several old-fashioned favorites that you're sure to enjoy again — especially since our versions are quicker and easier than ever. For many of these sumptuous creations, we just dressed up purchased mixes and turned something simple into a satiny smooth sensation!

NET WT
3.9 OZ
(110g)

47

DEATH BY CHOCOLATE

1 package (21.2 ounces) brownie mix
½ cup vegetable oil
2 eggs
¼ cup water
¼ cup coffee-flavored liqueur *or* 4 tablespoons strongly brewed coffee and 1 teaspoon sugar
3 packages (3.9 ounces each) chocolate instant pudding mix
6 cups milk
½ teaspoon almond extract
1 container (12 ounces) frozen non-dairy whipped topping, thawed
1 package (9 ounces) snack-size chocolate-covered toffee candy bars, crushed and divided

Chocolate curls to garnish

Preheat oven to 350 degrees. Prepare brownie mix with oil, eggs, and water in a large bowl according to package directions. Spread batter into a greased 9 x 13-inch baking pan and bake 24 to 26 minutes. Use a wooden skewer to poke holes about 1 inch apart in top of warm brownies; drizzle with liqueur. Cool completely.

Prepare pudding mixes with milk in a large bowl according to package directions; set aside. In a medium bowl, fold almond extract into whipped topping; set aside. In 4-quart serving bowl, break half of brownies into bite-size pieces. Sprinkle half of crushed candy bars over brownies. Spread half of pudding over candy pieces. Spread half of whipped topping mixture over pudding layer. Repeat layers, ending with whipped topping mixture. Cover and chill. Garnish with chocolate curls.

Yield: about 20 servings

Favor special guests with our decadent Death By Chocolate. Layers of bite-size mocha brownie pieces are alternated with chocolate-covered toffee bits, instant chocolate pudding, and almond-kissed whipped topping. Crowned with chocolate curls, this dessert is to die for!

Buttermilk baking mix provides a quick start to Chocolate Cream Crêpes (left). An elegant ending to dinner, the crêpes are folded around a smooth chocolate-cream cheese filling. Prepared using pudding mix and marshmallow creme, luscious Mocha Chocolate Cream is laced with coffee-flavored liqueur.

CHOCOLATE CREAM CRÊPES

- 1 cup buttermilk baking mix
- 3/4 cup milk
- 2 eggs
- 1 package (3 ounces) cream cheese, softened
- 1/2 tablespoons cocoa
- 6 tablespoons sugar
- 1/2 cup sour cream
- 1/2 teaspoon vanilla extract

  Whipped cream and cocoa to garnish

Combine baking mix, milk, and eggs in a medium bowl; beat until smooth. Place a lightly greased 8-inch skillet over medium heat. For each crêpe, spoon about 2 tablespoons batter into heated skillet. Tilt skillet to spread batter evenly over bottom of pan to form about a 5 1/2-inch circle. Cook until lightly browned; turn over and cook about 30 seconds. Place between layers of waxed paper.

In a medium bowl, beat cream cheese, 1 1/2 tablespoons cocoa, and sugar until fluffy. Beat in sour cream and vanilla. Spread 1 tablespoon filling along center of each crêpe; fold edges of crêpe over filling. Garnish with whipped cream; sift cocoa over crêpes.

Yield: about 14 crêpes

MOCHA CHOCOLATE CREAM

- 2 cups milk
- 1 1/2 tablespoons instant coffee granules
- 1 package (3.4 ounces) chocolate pudding mix
- 1 jar (7 ounces) marshmallow creme
- 2 tablespoons coffee-flavored liqueur

  Chocolate curls to garnish

In a large saucepan, combine milk and instant coffee; stir in pudding mix. Stirring frequently, cook over medium heat until mixture comes to a full boil. Remove from heat. Add marshmallow creme and liqueur; stir until well blended. Spoon into serving dishes. Cover and chill. Garnish with chocolate curls.

Yield: about 7 servings

49

Canned fruit is simply stirred into vanilla pudding for Creamy Pineapple-Orange Dessert. Spooned over packaged ladyfingers, this chilled concoction is deliciously different!

CREAMY PINEAPPLE-ORANGE DESSERT

2 cans (11 ounces each) mandarin oranges, drained and divided
1 package (3 ounces) vanilla pudding mix
2 cups milk
1 can (8 ounces) crushed pineapple, drained
1 package (3 ounces) ladyfingers (about 12 ladyfingers)

Reserve several mandarin orange slices for garnish. Combine pudding mix and milk in a medium saucepan. Stirring constantly, cook over medium heat until mixture comes to a full boil. Remove from heat; stir in pineapple and remaining oranges. Cool to room temperature.

Cut ladyfingers in half crosswise. Line sides of a 9 x 2-inch-deep round baking dish with pieces. Cut remaining ladyfingers in half lengthwise and place on bottom of dish. Spread pudding mixture over ladyfingers in bottom of dish. Garnish with reserved orange slices. Cover and chill 1 hour or until firm.

Yield: about 8 servings

TAPIOCA-PEACH PARFAITS

2³/₄ cups milk
¹/₃ cup sugar
3 tablespoons quick-cooking tapioca
1 egg, beaten

teaspoon almond extract

can (21 ounces) peach pie filling,
    chilled

tablespoons amaretto

Toasted sliced almonds to garnish

a medium saucepan, combine milk,
r, tapioca, and egg; let stand 5 minutes.
ring constantly, cook over medium heat
l mixture begins to boil. Remove from
; stir in almond extract. Pour into a
dium bowl and place plastic wrap
ctly on surface; chill about 30 minutes
ntil mixture thickens.
ombine pie filling and amaretto in a
ll bowl. In 4 parfait glasses, alternately
r tapioca pudding with pie filling
ture, ending with pie filling mixture.
nish with almonds.

ld: 4 servings

OCONUT-BANANA PUDDING

1   package (3.4 ounces) coconut
        cream instant pudding mix

2   cups milk

1   banana, mashed

2   tablespoons flaked coconut

2   bananas

4   vanilla wafers, broken into large
        pieces

    Banana slices, chopped pecans,
        and coconut to serve

In a medium bowl, add pudding mix to
lk; beat until thickened. Stir in mashed
nana and 2 tablespoons coconut. Slice
ananas. Layer vanilla wafer pieces,
nana slices, and pudding in 6 individual
ving dishes. Cover and chill until ready to
ve. To serve, place banana slices, pecans,
d coconut over pudding.

ld: 6 servings

Amaretto liqueur adds excitement to Tapioca-Peach Parfaits (top), layered desserts made with peach pie filling and quick-cooking tapioca. A tasty twist on a Southern favorite, Coconut-Banana Pudding combines flaked coconut and mellow bananas with instant coconut cream pudding.

51

Fruity Apple Bread Pudding begins with unseasoned croutons that are soaked in a mixture of milk, applesauce, and spices. Packed with walnuts and raisins, the baked pudding is served with a caramel-whiskey sauce made with purchased ice cream topping.

APPLE BREAD PUDDING

- 2 cups milk
- 1 cup applesauce
- 3/4 cup sugar
- 2 eggs
- 1 teaspoon vanilla extract
- 1 teaspoon apple pie spice
- 1 teaspoon ground cinnamon
- 1 package (5 ounces) unseasoned croutons (about 2 1/2 cups)
- 1 cup chopped walnuts
- 1/4 cup raisins
- 1 container (12.5 ounces) caramel ice cream topping
- 3 tablespoons whiskey

Preheat oven to 350 degrees. Whisk first 7 ingredients in a large bowl. Stir in croutons, walnuts, and raisins; allow to stand 10 minutes. Pour into a greased 9-inch square baking pan. Bake 50 to 55 minutes or until a knife inserted in center of bread pudding comes out clear. Allow to stand 10 minutes before serving.

Pour caramel topping into a small saucepan. Bring to a boil over medium-h heat. Remove from heat; stir in whiskey. Serve warm sauce over bread pudding.

Yield: about 9 servings

CUSTARD WITH CARAMEL-PEC TOPPING

- 2 cups evaporated milk
- 4 eggs
- 4 tablespoons firmly packed brown sugar
- 1 tablespoon vanilla extract
- 1 container (12.5 ounces) caramel ice cream topping
- 1/2 cup chopped pecans

Preheat oven to 325 degrees. In a medium bowl, whisk evaporated milk, eggs, brown sugar, and vanilla. Pour into 6 ungreased 6-ounce custard cups. Place

Reward your taste buds with these old-fashioned favorites! Custard with Caramel-Pecan Topping (left) is a basic ~~ssert~~ that's prepared with only four ingredients and drenched with a rich, nutty sauce. Custard mix makes Homestyle ~~ce~~ Pudding a no-fuss delight. The creamy treat is loaded with plump raisins.

~~ps~~ in a 9 x 13-inch baking pan. Place pan ~~~~ oven and fill with hot water about halfway ~~•~~ sides of cups. Bake 30 to 35 minutes or ~~til~~ a knife inserted in center of custard ~~mes~~ out clean. Remove cups from water. ~~low~~ custard to cool 10 minutes before ~~moving~~ from cups.

~~Combine~~ caramel topping and pecans in ~~small~~ saucepan. Stirring constantly, bring ~~~~ a boil over medium heat. Remove from ~~at.~~

To serve, loosen edges of custard with a knife. Invert onto dessert plates. Spoon warm caramel topping over warm custard.

Yield: 6 servings

HOMESTYLE RICE PUDDING

  3 cups milk
  1 egg yolk, beaten
  1 package (4.4 ounces) custard mix
$^1/_2$ cup raisins, divided
  1 cup cooked rice

In a medium saucepan, combine milk and egg yolk; stir in custard mix. Stirring constantly, bring to a boil over medium heat. Remove from heat. Reserving 2 tablespoons raisins for garnish, stir in rice and remaining raisins. Spoon into serving dishes. Cover and chill. Garnish with reserved raisins.

Yield: about 4 servings

Extra-easy Citrus Trifle (left) *layers a fluffy mixture of instant pudding and fruit with bites of purchased pound cake. The dessert is crowned with orange-flavored whipped topping and toasted coconut. Vanilla and chocolate pudding mixes are time-savers when making Layered Chocolate-Almond Delight.*

CITRUS TRIFLE

1 can (15¼ ounces) pineapple
     tidbits
2 packages (3.4 ounces each)
     vanilla instant pudding mix
3 cups milk
1 container (8 ounces) sour cream
1 can (11 ounces) mandarin
     oranges, drained
1 purchased pound cake
     (16 ounces), cut into bite-size
     pieces

1 container (8 ounces) frozen non-
     dairy whipped topping, thawed
2 tablespoons orange-flavored
     liqueur
   Toasted flaked coconut
     to garnish

Drain pineapple, reserving juice. Combine pudding mixes, milk, and ½ cup reserved pineapple juice in a medium bowl. Beat until well blended. Fold in sour cream, oranges, and drained pineapple. Layer one-third of cake pieces in a 3-quart serving bowl; drizzle with one-third of remaining reserved pineapple juice. Spoon one-third of pudding mixture over cake. Repeat layers twice, ending with pudding mixture. Cover and chill at least 3 hours.

To serve, combine whipped topping and liqueur; spread over top of trifle. Garnish with toasted coconut.

Yield: 12 to 14 servings

ERED CHOCOLATE-ALMOND
LIGHT

cup all-purpose flour
tablespoons granulated sugar
cup butter or margarine
cup sliced almonds, chopped
package (8 ounces) cream cheese,
    softened
cup sifted confectioners sugar
container (8 ounces) frozen non-
    dairy whipped topping, thawed
    and divided
package (3.9 ounces) chocolate
    instant pudding mix
cups milk, divided
package (3.4 ounces) vanilla
    instant pudding mix
milk chocolate candy bars with
    almonds (1.45 ounces each),
    chopped, to garnish

reheat oven to 350 degrees. In a
ium bowl, combine flour and
ulated sugar. Using a pastry blender
knives, cut in butter until mixture
mbles coarse meal. Stir in almonds.
s into bottom of a 9 x 13-inch baking
. Bake 15 to 17 minutes or until edges
lightly browned. Cool in dish on a wire

a medium bowl, beat cream cheese
confectioners sugar until fluffy. Fold in
p whipped topping. Spread over cooled
st. In a small bowl, add chocolate
ding mix to 1¹/₃ cups milk; beat until
kened. Spread pudding over cream
ese mixture layer. In another small
l, add vanilla pudding mix to remaining
cups milk; beat until thickened. Spread
lla pudding over chocolate pudding.
er and chill 15 minutes or until firm.
o serve, spread remaining whipped
ping over vanilla pudding. Garnish with
pped candy bars. Cut into 2¹/₂-inch
ares.

d: about 12 servings

Individual Cherry Bread Cups are quick to prepare with maraschino cherries and cubed white bread. A warm pudding and dollops of whipped topping add the finishing touches.

CHERRY BREAD CUPS

2 jars (6 ounces each) maraschino
    cherries, divided
4 slices white bread, cubed
¹/₂ cup sugar
2 eggs, beaten
2 tablespoons butter or margarine,
    melted
1 tablespoon all-purpose flour
1 package (3 ounces) vanilla
    pudding mix
2 cups milk
    Frozen non-dairy whipped
    topping, thawed, to garnish

Preheat oven to 375 degrees. Drain cherries, reserving juice; add enough water to cherry juice to make ²/₃ cup. Coarsely chop cherries. Combine ¹/₂ cup cherries, reserved juice mixture, bread cubes, sugar, eggs, melted butter, and flour in a small bowl. Spoon mixture evenly into 6 greased 6-ounce custard cups. Place cups in a 9 x 13-inch baking pan. Place pan in oven and fill with hot water about halfway up sides of cups. Bake 25 to 30 minutes or until edges of mixture begin to pull away from sides of cups.

While bread cups are baking, add pudding mix to milk in a medium saucepan. Stirring constantly, cook over medium heat until mixture comes to a full boil. Remove from heat. Stir in remaining cherries.

To serve, spoon warm pudding mixture over each bread cup. Garnish with whipped topping. Serve warm.

Yield: 6 servings

CREAMY BLUEBERRY SQUARE

1¼ cups all-purpose flour
½ cup firmly packed brown sugar
½ cup butter or margarine, softene
½ cup chopped pecans
1 package (8 ounces) cream chees
softened
¾ cup granulated sugar
2 eggs
1 can (21 ounces) blueberry pie
filling
2 teaspoons lemon juice

Frozen non-dairy whipped
topping, thawed, to garnish

Preheat oven to 350 degrees. For cru
combine flour, brown sugar, butter, and
pecans in a medium bowl. Press mixture
into bottom of a 9 x 13-inch baking pan
a medium bowl, beat cream cheese,
granulated sugar, and eggs until smooth.
Pour cream cheese mixture over crust.
Bake 20 to 25 minutes or until filling is
and begins to brown around the edges.
in pan 15 minutes on a wire rack.

Combine pie filling and lemon juice i
small bowl. Spread blueberry mixture ov
cream cheese filling. Cover and chill.

To serve, cut into 2-inch squares.
Garnish with whipped topping.

Yield: about 24 servings

BROWNIE CRÈME BRÛLÉE

1 package (21.5 ounces) brownie
mix
4 eggs, lightly beaten
½ cup brewed coffee
¼ cup vegetable oil
½ cup firmly packed brown sugar
2 tablespoons butter, softened

Preheat oven to 350 degrees. In a
medium bowl, combine brownie mix, eg
coffee, and oil; stir just until blended. Po
batter into 6 lightly greased 6-ounce

Creamy Blueberry Squares feature a buttery brown sugar crust covered with sweetened cream cheese and canned pie filling.

Here's how to finish a meal with flair! Rich mocha-flavored sensations, our individual servings of Brownie Crème *brûlée* (left) *have the signature caramelized tops. Packaged brownie mix makes the choice offering a breeze to create.* *ou'll savor the flavor of Cherry Cream Cheese Dessert. It's a simple mixture of cream cheese, sweetened condensed milk,* *d canned pie filling.*

ekins. Place ramekins in a 9 x 13-inch
ing pan. Place pan in oven and fill with
water halfway up sides of ramekins.
e 34 to 36 minutes. Place ramekins on
ire rack to cool while preparing
ping.
n a small bowl, combine brown sugar
butter until crumbly. Sprinkle about
blespoon mixture over each warm
sert. Place ramekins on a baking sheet
ches from broiler and broil about 2 to

3 minutes or until sugar caramelizes.
Serve warm.

Yield: 6 servings

CHERRY CREAM CHEESE DESSERT

1 package (8 ounces) cream cheese,
  softened
1 can (14 ounces) sweetened
  condensed milk
⅓ cup lemon juice

1 teaspoon vanilla extract
1 can (21 ounces) cherry pie filling
  Toasted slivered almonds to
    garnish

In a large bowl, beat cream cheese until
fluffy. Beat in sweetened condensed milk,
lemon juice, and vanilla. Lightly swirl pie
filling into cream cheese mixture. Spoon
into serving dishes. Cover and chill. Garnish
with almonds.

Yield: about 6 servings

SHORT & SWEET BREADS

The aroma of freshly baked bread hypnotizes the senses and automatically draws the family to the kitchen. Moist, delicious loaves, nut-filled muffins, and delightfully sticky buns are only a few of the mouth-watering treats that await you in our tempting assortment of fast-to-fix sweet breads. They're perfect for perking up breakfast, satisfying a snack attack, or curbing a craving for something sweet. Prepared with packaged mixes, refrigerated rolls, and just a few simple ingredients, these easy oven offerings will make you fall in love with baking all over again!

Pineapple-Pumpkin Bread	Orange-Date-Nut Loaves
Raspberry-Chocolate Danish Squares	Butterscotch Bran Muffins
Nut Muffins	Cinnamon-Orange Sticky Buns
Golden Monkey Bread	Streusel Muffins
Peanut Butter and Jelly Muffins	Dandy Doughnuts
Dessert Waffles	Pineapple Upside-Down Cinnamon Rolls

PINEAPPLE-PUMPKIN BREAD

1 package (16 ounces) pound cake
    mix
2 teaspoons pumpkin pie spice
1 teaspoon baking soda
1 cup canned pumpkin
1 can (8 ounces) crushed
    pineapple
2 eggs
1 cup chopped pecans

Preheat oven to 325 degrees. Grease
bottoms of two 4$1/2$ x 8$1/2$-inch loaf pans
and line bottoms with waxed paper. Grea
and flour waxed paper and sides of pans.
a large bowl, combine cake mix, pumpki
pie spice, and baking soda. Add pumpki
undrained pineapple, and eggs; beat unti
well blended. Stir in pecans. Spoon batte
into prepared pans. Bake 45 to 55 minut
or until a toothpick inserted in center of
bread comes out clean. Cool in pans
20 minutes. Remove from pans and serve
warm or cool completely on a wire rack.

Yield: 2 loaves bread

RASPBERRY-CHOCOLATE DANI
SQUARES

1 package (8 ounces) cream cheese
    softened
$1/2$ cup seedless raspberry jam,
    divided
1 package (18.25 ounces)
    chocolate fudge cake mix with
    pudding in the mix, divided
3 eggs
1$1/2$ cups sour cream
1 tablespoon butter or margarine
$1/2$ cup slivered almonds
$2/3$ cup sifted confectioners sugar
2 to 3 teaspoons water
$1/4$ teaspoon vanilla extract

Here's a delicious mid-morning snack or coffee break treat! Pineapple-Pumpkin Bread is prepared with pound cake mix, canned pumpkin, and crushed pineapple and loaded with chopped pecans.

Chocolate fudge cake mix helps make Raspberry-Chocolate Danish Squares (left) *irresistible! The extra-moist pastries [fea]ture wells of fruity jam, a sprinkling of almonds, and a drizzling of icing. Bursting with pecans, miniature Nut [Mu]ffins are quick to make using pantry staples.*

[P]reheat oven to 350 degrees. Combine [crea]m cheese and 2 tablespoons raspberry [jam] in a small bowl. Reserve ¹/₂ cup dry [cak]e mix in another small bowl. In a [med]ium bowl, lightly beat eggs. Stir in sour [crea]m and remaining cake mix (mixture [will] be slightly lumpy). Spread mixture in a [grea]sed 10¹/₂ x 15¹/₂ x 1-inch jellyroll pan. [In 1]8 evenly-spaced places, spoon about [1 te]aspoons cream cheese mixture on top of [batt]er. Use a pastry blender or 2 knives to [cut] butter into reserved cake mix until [mixt]ure resembles coarse meal. Stir in [alm]onds. Sprinkle mixture over batter. Bake [20 t]o 25 minutes or until a toothpick [inse]rted in cake comes out clean. Place

about 1 teaspoon raspberry jam in each indentation in cake. In a small bowl, combine confectioners sugar, water, and vanilla; stir until smooth. Drizzle icing over top. Cut into 18 squares; serve warm.

Yield: 18 servings

NUT MUFFINS

1¹/₂ cups firmly packed brown sugar
1¹/₂ cups chopped pecans
 ¹/₂ cup all-purpose flour
 ¹/₈ teaspoon salt
  3   eggs, beaten
 ¹/₂ teaspoon vanilla extract
       Vegetable cooking spray

In a medium bowl, combine brown sugar, pecans, flour, and salt. Stir in eggs and vanilla just until blended (batter will be lumpy). Heavily spray miniature muffin cups with cooking spray. Fill cups about two-thirds full. Place muffin pans in a cold oven. Set temperature on 300 degrees and bake 25 minutes. Cool on a wire rack 1 minute; run a knife gently around edge of each muffin cup to loosen muffins. Allow to sit in pan another 5 minutes; transfer muffins to a wire rack to cool completely.

Yield: about 3 dozen mini muffins

Served warm from the oven, Golden Monkey Bread will please the palate with a cinnamony butterscotch-pecan glaz Frozen dinner rolls make this gooey creation simple to bake.

GOLDEN MONKEY BREAD

 1 cup firmly packed brown sugar
 1 teaspoon ground cinnamon
 1 package (25 ounces) frozen
   white dinner yeast rolls, thawed
 1/2 cup butter or margarine, melted
 1/2 cup butterscotch chips, divided
 1/2 cup chopped pecans, divided

In a small bowl, combine brown sugar and cinnamon. Tear each roll into 3 pieces.

Dip each piece into melted butter and roll in brown sugar mixture. Place half of dough pieces in a greased 10-inch fluted tube pan. Sprinkle 1/4 cup butterscotch chips and 1/4 cup pecans over dough. Place remaining dough pieces in pan. Sprinkle remaining butterscotch chips and pecans over dough. Cover and let rise in a warm place (80 to 85 degrees) about 2 1/2 hours or until doubled in size.

Preheat oven to 375 degrees. Bake 25 30 minutes or until golden brown. Cover with aluminum foil if bread begins to bro too quickly. Cool in pan 10 minutes. Inve bread onto a serving plate. Serve warm.

Yield: 10 to 12 servings

PEANUT BUTTER AND JELLY MUFFINS

1 package (18.25 ounces) white
    cake mix
1 teaspoon baking soda
1 cup crunchy peanut butter
4 cup water
2 eggs
3 cup strawberry jam

Preheat oven to 350 degrees. In a large
bowl, combine cake mix and baking soda.
Add peanut butter, water, and eggs; beat just
until blended. Fill paper-lined muffin cups
about two-thirds full. Place a teaspoonful of
jam in center of batter in each muffin cup.
Bake 18 to 23 minutes or until a toothpick
inserted in muffin comes out clean. Serve
warm.

Yield: about 1½ dozen muffins

DESSERT WAFFLES

1 cup pancake and waffle mix
2 tablespoons sugar
¾ cup water
1 egg
2 tablespoons butter or margarine,
    melted
½ teaspoon vanilla extract
    Vanilla ice cream and strawberry
    ice cream topping to serve

Preheat a Belgian waffle iron. In a
medium bowl, combine waffle mix and
sugar. Add water, egg, melted butter, and
vanilla; stir just until blended. For each
waffle, pour about ½ cup batter into waffle
iron. Bake 3 to 5 minutes or according to
manufacturer's instructions until done.
Serve warm waffles with ice cream and
strawberry topping.

Yield: about 4 waffles

Peanut Butter and Jelly Muffins (top) *are sure to please kids of all ages! The jam-filled sweets are prepared from a cake mix and flavored with crunchy peanut butter. A little sugar and vanilla are all it takes to turn ordinary breakfast fare into yummy Dessert Waffles.*

ORANGE-DATE-NUT LOAVES

1 package (16 ounces) pound cake
   mix
2/3 cup vegetable oil
1/2 cup sweetened condensed milk
2 eggs
1 teaspoon orange extract
2 cups chopped pecans
1 package (8 ounces) chopped
   dates

Preheat oven to 325 degrees. In a larg
bowl, beat cake mix, oil, sweetened
condensed milk, eggs, and orange extrac
low speed of an electric mixer 30 secon
Beat at medium speed 2 minutes. Stir in
pecans and dates. Spoon batter into
2 greased and floured 5 x 9-inch loaf pa
Bake 1 hour to 1 hour 10 minutes or un
toothpick inserted in center of bread cor
out with only a few crumbs attached. Coc
pans 10 minutes. Remove from pans and
cool completely on a wire rack.

Yield: 2 loaves bread

BUTTERSCOTCH BRAN MUFFIN

1/2 cup butterscotch chips
4 ounces cream cheese
   Vegetable cooking spray
1 package (7 ounces) bran muffin
   mix
1/3 cup milk
1 egg, beaten

In a small saucepan, melt butterscotch
chips over low heat. Stir in cream cheese
until well blended; remove from heat.
Preheat oven to 400 degrees. Line 9 c
of a muffin pan with paper muffin cups;
spray paper cups with cooking spray. In
medium bowl, combine muffin mix, milk
egg, and half of butterscotch mixture; mi
just until moistened. Spoon batter into
prepared muffin cups, filling each about
two-thirds full. Bake 15 to 18 minutes or

*Using packaged mixes lets you serve up these heartwarming breads in a
flash! Pound cake mix is enhanced with pecans, dates, and orange extract to
create Orange-Date-Nut Loaf (left). Cream cheese makes Butterscotch Bran
Muffins extra moist and flavorful.*

Wake up breakfast, brunch, or a coffee break with oven-fresh Cinnamon-Orange Sticky Buns! The melt-in-your-mouth [bun]s are drenched in a buttery brown sugar topping that's enhanced with orange marmalade and chopped pecans.

[unti]l a toothpick inserted in center of muffin [com]es out clean. Cool in pan 10 minutes; [tran]sfer muffins to a wire rack. Spread [rem]aining butterscotch mixture over tops of [war]m muffins. Serve warm.

[Yiel]d: 9 muffins

CINNAMON-ORANGE STICKY BUNS

2 cans (11.5 ounces each) refrigerated cinnamon rolls with icing
1/2 cup orange marmalade
3 tablespoons chopped pecans
1 cup firmly packed brown sugar
1/3 cup butter or margarine, melted

Preheat oven to 350 degrees. In a small bowl, combine icing from cinnamon roll cans, marmalade, and pecans; spread in bottom of a greased 10-inch fluted tube pan. Place brown sugar in another small bowl. Dip each roll into melted butter and roll in brown sugar. Stand rolls on ends in pan. Sprinkle with remaining brown sugar. Bake 35 to 40 minutes or until golden brown. Cool in pan 5 minutes. Invert onto a serving plate. Serve warm.

Yield: 16 sticky buns

Cater to your sweet tooth with these tasty goodies. Streusel Muffins (left) have the appeal of cinnamon, pecans, and apples baked right in. Prepared with a cake mix, they're completed with a drizzling of cream cheese frosting. Glazed w a simple icing, Dandy Doughnuts are as fun to make as they are to eat! The light pastries are simple to cut from canne biscuits, and the tiny holes are bite-size delights.

STREUSEL MUFFINS

STREUSEL

- 5 tablespoons firmly packed brown sugar
- 2 tablespoons all-purpose flour
- 1¼ teaspoons ground cinnamon
- 2 tablespoons butter or margarine
- ⅓ cup chopped pecans

MUFFINS

- 1 package (18.25 ounces) yellow cake mix
- ¾ cup applesauce
- 3 eggs
- ½ cup vegetable oil
- ½ cup cream cheese ready-to-spread frosting

Preheat oven to 350 degrees. For streusel, combine brown sugar, flour, and cinnamon in a small bowl. Using a pastry blender or 2 knives, cut in butter until mixture is crumbly. Stir in pecans.

For muffins, combine cake mix, applesauce, eggs, and oil in a large bowl; beat just until blended. Spoon about 1½ tablespoons batter into each paper-lined muffin cup. Sprinkle 1 teaspoon streusel over batter. Repeat with remaini batter and streusel. Bake 18 to 23 minute or until a toothpick inserted in center of muffin comes out clean. Cool in pan 5 minutes. Transfer muffins to a wire rac with waxed paper underneath.

In a small microwave-safe bowl, microwave frosting on high power (100% 15 to 25 seconds or until frosting melts. Drizzle frosting over warm muffins. Serve warm.

Yield: about 1½ dozen muffins

NDY DOUGHNUTS

cups sifted confectioners sugar
tablespoons water
teaspoon vanilla extract
Vegetable oil
can (10-count) refrigerated
 biscuits

a small bowl, combine confectioners
r, water, and vanilla; stir until smooth.
a heavy medium saucepan, heat 1 to
inches oil over medium-high heat.
g the middle of a doughnut cutter or a
l round cookie cutter, cut out centers
scuits. Fry doughnuts and holes in oil
 lightly browned on both sides; drain
aper towels.
p hot doughnuts and holes into glaze
place on a wire rack with waxed paper
erneath. Serve warm.

d: 10 doughnuts and 10 doughnut holes

EAPPLE UPSIDE-DOWN
NAMON ROLLS

can (15¼ ounces) crushed
 pineapple, drained
cup firmly packed brown sugar
tablespoons butter
can (11.5 ounces) refrigerated
 cinnamon rolls
Maraschino cherry halves to
 garnish

reheat oven to 375 degrees. Place
apple, brown sugar, and butter in a
²-inch heavy ovenproof skillet. Place
et in oven 10 minutes or until butter
s. Remove skillet from oven; stir
apple mixture to blend. Place rolls on
of pineapple mixture. Bake in lower half
ven 16 to 18 minutes or until rolls are
tly browned. Immediately invert onto a
ing plate. Garnish with cherry halves.
e warm.

d: 8 cinnamon rolls

Garnished with maraschino cherries, Pineapple Upside-Down Cinnamon Rolls have the familiar flavor of a classic cake, but they're so much easier to make! Just bake refrigerated cinnamon rolls in a brown sugar-pineapple mixture and enjoy.

FAST & FRUITY

*In the good old summertime, fresh fruit abounds!
The mouth-watering goodness of a ripe and juicy harvest
inspires a banquet of fruit-filled desserts to liven up any
occasion. From extra-quick seasonal sundaes to "berry"
delicious dessert pizzas, our sun-kissed selections will
tantalize your taste buds with their natural sweetness.
Purchased pastries, flavored gelatins, refrigerated doughs,
and, of course, Mother Nature's own bountiful offerings
make these warm-weather desserts sweet, wholesome
treats that your entire family can enjoy.*

A lemon-cream cheese filling with a confetti of sliced fruit offers a delicious complement to extra-moist cake in Summer Fruit Dessert. Cake and pudding mixes help you create this luscious treat without a lot of fuss.

SUMMER FRUIT DESSERT

CAKE

1 package (18.25 ounces) lemon cake mix with pudding in the mix

1 cup water

3 eggs

1 package (3 ounces) cream cheese, softened

FILLING

1 package (3 ounces) cream cheese, softened

1½ cups milk, divided

1 package (3.4 ounces) lemon instant pudding mix

1 teaspoon grated lemon zest

1½ cups frozen non-dairy whipped topping, thawed and divided

1½ cups sliced fresh fruit, divided (we used peaches, strawberries, and kiwi fruit)

Preheat oven to 350 degrees. For cake, combine cake mix, water, eggs, and cream cheese in a large bowl. Beat at low speed of an electric mixer 30 seconds. Beat at medium speed 2 minutes. Pour into a greased 10-inch fluted tube pan. Bake 45-50 minutes or until a toothpick inserted in center of cake comes out clean. Cool in pan 15 minutes. Invert onto a wire rack and cool completely.

Place cake on a serving plate. Make a horizontal cut through cake about 2 inches from bottom; set top of cake aside. Use a

to pull out interior of cake, leaving
...t a ³/₄-inch shell on sides and bottom
...ake.

...or filling, beat cream cheese in a large
...l until smooth. Gradually add 1 cup
..., beating until well blended. Add
...ding mix, lemon zest, and remaining
...up milk; beat until thickened. Fold in
...up whipped topping. Spread about half
...lling into bottom of cake. Place about
...p fruit slices over filling. Spread
...aining filling over fruit slices. Replace
...e top. Spread remaining whipped
...ing on cake. Place remaining fruit
...es on whipped topping. Serve
...ediately.

...d: about 16 servings

...NTALOUPE-RASPBERRY
...NDAES

- 2 cantaloupes
- 1 pint fresh red raspberries
- 1 pint vanilla ice cream
- ...₄ cup purchased melba sauce

     Fresh mint leaves to garnish

...ut each cantaloupe in half crosswise.
... a thin slice from bottom of each
...taloupe half so it will sit flat. Leaving
...ut a ³/₄-inch shell, use a melon baller to
...op flesh from cantaloupes. Use a spoon
...coop out additional flesh to smooth
...des of cantaloupes. In a medium bowl,
...bine melon balls and raspberries. Place
...nall scoops of ice cream in each melon
...f. Top with fruit mixture. Drizzle with
...lba sauce. Garnish with mint leaves.
...ve immediately.

...d: 4 servings

*Take advantage of tasty summer fruit — indulge in Cantaloupe-Raspberry
Sundaes! For these quick and cool creations, scoops of vanilla ice cream
are placed in cantaloupe halves, topped with berries and melon balls, and
drizzled with store-bought melba sauce.*

BLUEBERRY-LIME FROZEN DESSERT

  3 cups lime sherbet, softened
  3/4 cup crushed vanilla wafer crumbs
      (about 20 cookies)
  1 pint fresh blueberries

Place a layer of sherbet, cookie crumb and blueberries in 4 parfait glasses. Rep layers, ending with blueberries. Serve immediately.

Yield: 4 servings

FRESH ORANGE-PLUM ICE

  3 seedless oranges, peeled and cut
      into bite-size pieces
  1 pound fresh plums, quartered
  1 cup white grape juice
  1/2 cup port wine
  1/2 cup sugar
      Cinnamon stick
  1/2 teaspoon vanilla extract

In a medium saucepan, combine oranges, plums, grape juice, wine, sugar and cinnamon stick. Bring to a boil over medium-high heat. Cover saucepan and reduce heat to low, simmering about 15 minutes. Remove from heat. Remove cinnamon stick and place mixture in a fo processor. Add vanilla and pulse process until fruit is coarsely chopped and well blended. Pour into a nonmetal container Cover and freeze until firm.

To serve, remove from freezer and all to soften about 30 minutes.

Yield: about 5 cups fruit ice

It only takes minutes to create Blueberry-Lime Frozen Dessert (top), *a refreshing summertime ambrosia! It's made with layers of sherbet, cookie crumbs, and succulent blueberries and served in parfait glasses. Port wine and grape juice add sparkle to Fresh Orange-Plum Ice, a frosty pleaser flavored with cinnamon and fruit.*

Wake up the buffet with our colorful Fruit Fiesta! This tantalizing dessert pizza is prepared with a sweet crust made m refrigerated sugar cookie dough and topped with fluffy orange-cream cheese spread and fresh fruit.

UIT FIESTA

0 ounces refrigerated sugar cookie
    dough (¹/₂ of a 20-ounce
    package)
1 package (8 ounces) cream cheese,
    softened
✓₃ cup sugar
2 tablespoons plus 2 teaspoons
    orange-flavored liqueur, divided
✓₂ teaspoon vanilla extract

4 cups sliced fresh apricots,
    strawberries, bananas, and
    whole blueberries
¹/₄ cup apricot preserves

Preheat oven to 350 degrees. Press cookie dough into a greased 12-inch pizza pan. Bake 12 to 15 minutes or until dough is lightly browned. Cool pan on a wire rack.

In a medium bowl, beat cream cheese, sugar, 2 tablespoons liqueur, and vanilla until fluffy. Spread over cooled crust. Beginning at outer edge, arrange fruit slices over cream cheese mixture. Melt apricot preserves in a small saucepan over low heat. Remove from heat. Stir in remaining 2 teaspoons liqueur. Brush over fruit. Cover and chill 30 minutes. Cut into wedges to serve.

Yield: about 12 servings

Elegant and extra easy to prepare, Berry Combo (left) *presents a compote of plump, juicy berries that's marinated in light cinnamon-ginger syrup and then spooned into purchased puff pastry shells. Lemon Fruit Dip is a breeze to stir together with cream cheese, yogurt, and whipped topping.*

BERRY COMBO

1 cup fresh whole strawberries
1 cup fresh blueberries
1 cup fresh red raspberries
1 cup fresh blackberries
2 teaspoons cornstarch
2 tablespoons cold water
1 cup orange juice
1 tablespoon lemon juice
1 cup sugar
$^1/_2$ teaspoon ground cinnamon
$^1/_8$ teaspoon ground ginger
2 packages (10 ounces each) frozen puff pastry shells, baked according to package directions
Fresh berry leaves to garnish

In a large bowl, combine berries. In a small bowl, combine cornstarch and water.

In a medium saucepan, combine juices, sugar, cinnamon, and ginger; whisk until smooth. Stirring constantly, add cornstarch mixture and bring to a boil over medium-high heat. Reduce heat to medium and cook 6 minutes or until mixture begins to thicken. Remove from heat. Pour over berries and toss lightly. Cover and chill 1 hour.

To serve, spoon berry mixture into pastry shells. Garnish with berry leaves.

Yield: 12 servings

LEMON FRUIT DIP

1 package (3 ounces) cream cheese, softened
1 container (8 ounces) lemon yogurt
2 tablespoons sifted confectioners sugar
2 tablespoons lemon juice
1 container (8 ounces) frozen non-dairy whipped topping, thawed
Lemon slice and fresh berry leaves to garnish
Fresh fruit slices to serve

In a medium bowl, beat cream cheese until fluffy. Add yogurt, confectioners sugar, and lemon juice; beat until well blended. Fold in whipped topping. Garnish with lemon slice and berry leaves. Serve with fruit slices. Store in an airtight container in refrigerator.

Yield: about 4 cups dip

74

STRAWBERRIES AND BANANAS WITH SABAYON SAUCE

2 egg yolks
2 tablespoons sugar
2 tablespoons sweet Marsala wine
3 tablespoons orange juice
3 bananas, sliced
1 pint fresh strawberries, sliced

Combine egg yolks and sugar in the top of double boiler over simmering water. Whisking constantly, add wine and cook about 5 minutes or until mixture thickens. Transfer to a small bowl; cover and chill minutes.

In a medium bowl, sprinkle orange juice over banana slices. Add strawberries and toss lightly. To serve, spoon fruit mixture into serving dishes and top with chilled sauce.

Yield: about 5 servings

SPICED POACHED PEARS

6 medium fresh pears
1/4 cup water
1 tablespoon lemon juice
  Cinnamon stick, broken into
    3 pieces
6 cardamom pods, crushed
1/4 cup honey
1/4 cup butter or margarine
1/4 cup firmly packed brown sugar
  Fresh mint leaves to garnish

Leaving stems on fruit, peel pears. Core each pear from bottom almost to top, leaving stem end intact. Bring water, lemon juice, cinnamon stick pieces, and cardamom pods to a boil in a large saucepan over high heat. Place pears upright in water. Cover, reduce heat to medium, and simmer 15 to 25 minutes or until pears are tender. Remove pears from saucepan. Discard cinnamon, cardamom pods, and all but 1/4 cup liquid from

For a light and pleasing finish to any meal, try these unforgettable delights. Strawberries and Bananas with Sabayon Sauce (bottom) features fruit slices drenched in a creamy Marsala wine sauce. Tender Spiced Poached Pears are simmered with cinnamon and cardamom and served in a buttery honey sauce.

saucepan. Add honey, butter, and brown sugar to liquid over medium heat; stir until butter melts. Return pears to saucepan and cook 10 to 15 minutes or until sauce begins to thicken, spooning sauce over pears. Remove pears from sauce. Increase heat to medium-high. Stirring frequently, cook sauce about 4 minutes or until liquid is reduced and sauce is thickened. Spoon 1 tablespoon sauce into each of 6 serving dishes. Place pears on sauce. Spoon 1 teaspoon sauce over each pear. Garnish with mint leaves. Serve immediately.

Yield: 6 servings

PINEAPPLE PASSION

³/₄ cup boiling water
 1 package (3 ounces) orange-
     pineapple gelatin
 1 cup cold pineapple juice
 1 fresh pineapple
 1 cup whipping cream

Chill a small bowl and beaters from an electric mixer in freezer. In a large bowl, stir boiling water into gelatin until gelatin dissolves. Stir in pineapple juice. Cover and chill about 1 hour or until gelatin begins thicken.

Quarter pineapple, remove core, and remove most of fruit, reserving shells. Cut fruit into small pieces. Place fruit in a medium saucepan over medium heat and cook 8 minutes. Remove from heat; drain and allow to cool.

In chilled bowl, beat whipping cream until stiff peaks form. Reserving several pieces of pineapple for garnish, fold whipped cream and remaining pineapple into thickened gelatin. Chill 2 hours or un almost firm.

To serve, spoon mixture into pineappl shells. Garnish with reserved pineapple. Serve immediately.

Yield: 4 servings

BAKED CARAMEL APPLES

 6 large red baking apples (we used
     Rome Beauty apples)
2¹/₄ cups oatmeal cookie crumbs,
     divided
 ³/₄ cup caramel ice cream topping
 ¹/₄ cup apple juice

Preheat oven to 350 degrees. Core each apple almost to bottom of apple, leaving bottom intact. Using a vegetable peeler, remove a small strip of peel from top of each apple to prevent splitting. Place appl in an ungreased 7 x 11-inch baking dish.

You'll fall in love with Pineapple Passion! The chilled tropical treat is a blend of fresh pineapple, orange-pineapple gelatin, and whipping cream. For an eye-catching presentation, serve the dessert in pineapple "boats."

Our Baked Caramel Apples (bottom) *are sweet, tender perfection! A mixture of oatmeal cookie crumbs and caramel e cream topping is baked inside. A delicate delight, Frozen Fruit Fluff features fresh peaches and nectarines blended an airy lemon meringue.*

mbine 1¹/₂ cups cookie crumbs and
ramel topping in a small bowl. Spoon
okie crumb mixture into center of each
ple. Sprinkle remaining ³/₄ cup cookie
umbs over tops of apples. Pour apple
ce into baking dish. Bake 35 to
minutes or until apples are tender.
rve warm.

eld: 6 servings

FROZEN FRUIT FLUFF

    3 cups peeled, sliced ripe peaches
         and nectarines
1¹/₂ tablespoons lemon juice
    4 egg whites
 ¹/₂ cup sugar
         Peach and lemon slices and lemon
         zest strips to garnish

Process fruit slices and lemon juice in a
food processor until fruit is finely chopped.
In a large bowl, beat egg whites until soft
peaks form. Gradually add sugar to egg
whites, beating until stiff peaks form. Fold in
fruit mixture. Spoon into serving dishes.
Freeze until firm. Garnish with peach and
lemon slices and lemon zest.

Yield: about 7 servings

TROPICAL ANGEL DESSERT

- 1 package (3.4 ounces) French
    vanilla instant pudding mix
- 3 cups milk
- 1/2 teaspoon coconut extract
- 1/2 cup flaked coconut
- 1 10-inch angel food cake
- 1 to 2 carambola (star fruit), sliced
- 1 papaya, sliced
- 1 to 2 kiwi fruit, sliced
    Flaked coconut to garnish

In a medium bowl, add pudding mix t
milk and coconut extract; beat until
thickened. Stir in 1/2 cup coconut. Cover
and chill 30 minutes.

To serve, spoon pudding mixture over
slices of cake. Top with fruit slices. Garn
with coconut.

Yield: about 12 servings

STRAWBERRIES AND CREAM IN
PHYLLO CUPS

- 1 pint fresh strawberries
- 1 tablespoon granulated sugar
- 3 sheets frozen phyllo pastry, thawed
    Butter-flavored vegetable cooking
    spray
- 1 package (3 ounces) cream cheese
    softened
- 1/3 cup sour cream
- 1/4 cup sifted confectioners sugar
- 1 tablespoon vanilla extract

Slice strawberries into a small bowl. St
in granulated sugar; set aside.

Preheat oven to 375 degrees. Spray eac
sheet of pastry with cooking spray. Stack
pastry sheets together; cut into thirds
horizontally and vertically to make
9 rectangles (each small rectangle will ha
3 layers of pastry). Arrange layers in each
rectangle with points staggered. Place eac
set of pastry pieces in a muffin cup spraye

*Instant vanilla pudding is enhanced with coconut and served over slices
of angel food cake for our Tropical Angel Dessert. Simple and delicious, it's
topped with star fruit, papaya, and kiwi fruit.*

For an elegant yet easy ending to a brunch or light supper, serve Strawberries and Cream in Phyllo Cups (left). The flaky cups, made from frozen phyllo pastry, are a pleasing complement to the sweet, juicy fruit and creamy filling. Brimming with summery goodness, smooth Mango-Peach Cream is a yummy alternative to everyday desserts. This simple four-ingredient creation is quick to blend in the food processor.

th cooking spray. Bake 9 to 11 minutes or til lightly browned. Cool completely in n.

Transfer phyllo cups to a serving plate. In small bowl, beat cream cheese, sour eam, confectioners sugar, and vanilla til smooth. Spoon cream cheese mixture enly into phyllo cups. Top with awberries. Serve immediately.

eld: 9 servings

MANGO-PEACH CREAM

- 2 mangos, peeled and quartered
- 4 peaches, peeled and quartered
- 2/3 cup sweetened condensed milk
- 1 cup whipping cream
  Peach slices to garnish

Chill a small bowl and beaters from an electric mixer in freezer. Process fruit in a food processor until puréed. Add sweetened condensed milk and process until well blended. Cover and chill until ready to serve.

To serve, beat whipping cream in chilled bowl until stiff peaks form. Fold whipped cream into fruit mixture. Spoon into serving dishes and garnish with peach slices.

Yield: about 8 servings

COOL 'N' QUICK

Tangy fruit, mouth-watering chocolate, and refreshing mint are just a few of the delightful flavors you'll find in our tantalizing assortment of frozen confections. Store-bought ingredients such as ice cream, canned fruit, cake, and yogurt make it easy to whip up fabulous chilled desserts in no time at all. These treats are filled with guaranteed goodness that will have your friends and family asking for more!

Double Chocolate Ice Cream	Lemon Frozen Yogurt
Black Forest Angel Dessert	Chocolate Toffee Mud Pie
Tutti-Frutti Sherbet	Butterscotch Ice Cream Squares
Peachy Keen Cream	Chocolate Peppermint Cups
Tortilla Ice Cream Delights	Strawberry-Orange Frozen Yogurt
Apricot-Almond Ice Cream Pie	Ice Cream Sundae Cake

DOUBLE CHOCOLATE ICE CREAM

  6 chocolate-covered caramel and
      nougat candy bars (2.15 ounces
      each), cut into pieces
  ²/₃ cup sweetened condensed milk
  6 cups milk, divided
  ¹/₂ cup chocolate syrup

Place candy bar pieces and sweetened
condensed milk in a large microwave-safe
bowl. Microwave on high power (100%)
2 minutes or until mixture is smooth,
stirring after each minute. Stir in 2 cups
milk and chocolate syrup. Pour mixture in
a 4-quart ice cream freezer. Add remaining
4 cups milk. Freeze according to
manufacturer's instructions.

Yield: about 2 quarts ice cream

BLACK FOREST ANGEL DESSERT

  4 cups 1-inch cubes of angel food
      cake
  1 can (21 ounces) cherry pie filling
  1 quart chocolate ice cream,
      softened
  1 container (4 ounces) frozen non-
      dairy whipped topping, thawed
      Semisweet chocolate mini chips
      and maraschino cherry halves
      to garnish

Line a 5 x 9-inch loaf pan with plastic
wrap. Combine cake pieces and pie filling
in a large bowl. Spread half of ice cream in
bottom of prepared pan. Spoon cake
mixture over ice cream; top with remaining
ice cream. Cover and freeze until firm.

To serve, remove dessert from pan and
place on a serving dish. Spread whipped
topping over top and sides of dessert.
Garnish with chocolate chips and cherry
halves.

Yield: 8 to 10 servings

*Candy bars and chocolate syrup add up to fudgy goodness in Double
Chocolate Ice Cream. Served with chocolate-laced pirouette cookies, this
surprisingly easy dessert tastes like a million bucks!*

Garnished with maraschino cherries and miniature chocolate chips, Black Forest Angel Dessert (left) is an elegant but quick-to-make confection with chocolate ice cream, angel food cake, and cherry pie filling. Tutti-Frutti Sherbet, a "fun-tastic" blend of pineapples, cherries, and bananas, gets its tropical taste from fruit punch-flavored soft drink mix.

TUTTI-FRUTTI SHERBET

2²/₃ cups milk
1 can (5 ounces) evaporated milk
²/₃ cup sugar
1 package (0.16 ounces)
    unsweetened punch-flavored
    soft drink mix
¹/₈ teaspoon salt
1 jar (10 ounces) maraschino
    cherry halves, drained

1 can (8 ounces) crushed
    pineapple, drained
1 banana, sliced

In a large bowl, combine milks, sugar, soft drink mix, and salt. Stir until sugar dissolves. Stir in cherry halves, pineapple, and banana slices. Freeze in a 2-quart ice cream freezer according to manufacturer's instructions or cover and freeze until mixture is frozen 1 inch from sides of bowl; stir. Return to freezer until mixture is almost firm. Break up mixture with a spoon; beat with an electric mixer until well blended. Freeze until firm.

Yield: about 1³/₄ quarts sherbet

Summer-fresh flavor comes bursting through in Peachy Keen Cream (left), *a cool and refreshing dessert made with canned peaches, frozen orange juice, and whipped cream. Top off any fiesta with Tortilla Ice Cream Delights! The cinnamony treats layer sugared tortillas, dreamy ice cream, and rich caramel topping for an unbelievable taste sensati*

PEACHY KEEN CREAM

- 2 cans (16 ounces each) sliced peaches in heavy syrup
- 1 can (6 ounces) frozen orange juice concentrate, thawed
- 1/2 cup sugar
- 1 teaspoon vanilla extract
- 1 cup whipping cream, whipped

  Fresh mint leaves to garnish

Drain peaches, reserving 3/4 cup syrup. Combine peaches, reserved peach syrup, juice concentrate, sugar, and vanilla in a large bowl. Beat at low speed of an electric mixer until ingredients are combined and peaches are coarsely chopped. Fold whipped cream into peach mixture. Freeze in a 2-quart ice cream freezer according to manufacturer's instructions or cover and freeze 2 hours or until almost firm. Break up mixture with a spoon; beat with electric mixer until well blended. Freeze until firm. Garnish with mint leaves to serve.

Yield: about 1 1/2 quarts ice cream

TORTILLA ICE CREAM DELIGHTS

- 1/4 cup sugar
- 1 teaspoon ground cinnamon
  Vegetable oil
- 8 flour tortillas (about 6-inch diameter)
- 1 quart vanilla ice cream
- 1 container (12.5 ounces) caramel ice cream topping

Combine sugar and cinnamon in a small bowl. In a large skillet, heat 1/4 inch of oil over medium-high heat. Using a sharp knif

t small slits in centers of tortillas to help
ep them flat while frying. Lightly brown
th sides of tortillas in oil; drain on paper
wels. While still hot, sprinkle 1 side of
ch tortilla with 1 heaping teaspoon of
gar mixture. With sugar-coated side up,
nsfer to individual serving plates. Place
scoop ice cream on each tortilla. Drizzle
out 2 tablespoons caramel topping over
ch ice cream scoop.

eld: 8 servings

PRICOT-ALMOND
E CREAM PIE

1 cup graham cracker crumbs
1/4 cup butter or margarine, melted
3 tablespoons sugar
3/4 teaspoon almond extract
1/2 cup sliced almonds, toasted and
        divided
1 quart vanilla ice cream, softened
2/3 cup apricot preserves

Preheat oven to 350 degrees. Combine
acker crumbs, melted butter, sugar, and
mond extract in a small bowl. Stir in
cup almonds. Spread 1/4 cup cracker
umb mixture on an ungreased baking
eet. Bake 4 to 5 minutes or until slightly
unchy. Cool on pan; reserve for topping.
ess remaining cracker crumb mixture
to bottom of a greased 9-inch round cake
n. Spread about half of ice cream over
umb mixture. Spoon apricot preserves
er ice cream layer. Sprinkle with 1/8 cup
monds. Cover and freeze about
0 minutes. Spread a second layer of ice
eam over almonds. Sprinkle pie with
umb topping and remaining 1/8 cup
monds. Cover and freeze 1 to 11/2 hours
until firm. Remove from freezer
0 minutes before serving.

ield: about 8 servings

*Tangy apricot preserves give Apricot-Almond Ice Cream Pie its zesty flavor.
Toasted almonds, crunchy graham cracker crumbs, and smooth vanilla ice
cream offer a delightful contrast of textures.*

LEMON FROZEN YOGURT

¹/₂ cup sugar

1 envelope unflavored gelatin

1 cup skim milk

3 containers (8 ounces each) non-fat lemon yogurt

3¹/₂ tablespoons freshly squeezed lemon juice

Kiwi fruit slices to garnish

In a medium saucepan, combine sugar and gelatin; stir in milk and allow to stand 1 minute. Whisking constantly, cook over low heat 5 minutes or until gelatin dissolv Allow mixture to cool. Stir in yogurt and lemon juice. Freeze in a 2-quart ice crean freezer according to manufacturer's instructions or freeze in a large covered bowl overnight. Remove from freezer and allow to soften enough to be broken up w a spoon. Beat with an electric mixer until smooth; freeze until firm. Garnish with ki fruit slices.

Yield: about 1¹/₄ quarts frozen yogurt

CHOCOLATE TOFFEE MUD PIE

1 quart coffee ice cream, softened

4 bars (1.4 ounces each) chocolate-covered toffee, broken into bite-size pieces (about 1 cup)

1 purchased chocolate sandwich cookie pie crust (6 ounces)

1 container (12 ounces) fudge ice cream topping

2 tablespoons coffee-flavored liqueur

Toasted almond slices to garnish

In a medium bowl, combine ice cream and toffee pieces. Spoon into crust. Cover and freeze about 3 hours or until firm.

To serve, place fudge topping in a small microwave-safe bowl and microwave on high power (100%) 1 minute or until

Delectably light, Lemon Frozen Yogurt (top) *unites the tartness of lemon with the creamy goodness of yogurt for an utterly irresistible treat. Chocolate Toffee Mud Pie gets its mouth-watering taste from a winning combination of coffee ice cream, chocolate-covered toffee bars, fudge sauce, and coffee liqueur in a chocolate sandwich cookie crust.*

Quick-cooking oats and chopped pecans are certain to make Butterscotch Ice Cream Squares a family favorite. Children and adults both will go nuts over the sweet butterscotch crumb topping!

pping melts. Stir in liqueur. Spoon
ixture over each serving and garnish
th almond slices.

eld: about 8 servings

UTTERSCOTCH ICE CREAM QUARES

  1 cup all-purpose flour
$1/2$ cup butter or margarine, softened
$1/4$ cup firmly packed brown sugar
$1/4$ cup quick-cooking oats

$1/2$ cup chopped pecans
$1/2$ cup butterscotch ice cream
      topping, divided
  1 quart vanilla ice cream, softened

Preheat oven to 400 degrees. In a medium bowl, combine flour, butter, brown sugar, and oats until well blended. Stir in pecans. Spread mixture on an ungreased baking sheet. Stirring every 3 minutes, bake 12 to 15 minutes or until lightly browned. Cool on pan on a wire rack.

Crumble half of oat mixture into a lightly greased 8-inch square baking pan. Drizzle $1/4$ cup butterscotch topping over mixture. Spread ice cream over topping. Sprinkle remaining oat mixture over ice cream. Drizzle with remaining $1/4$ cup butterscotch topping. Cover and freeze $1 1/2$ to 2 hours or until firm. Remove from freezer 10 minutes before serving. Cut into 2-inch squares.

Yield: about 9 servings

Chocolate Peppermint Cups (left) *let you enjoy the classic taste of chocolate-mint with a unique twist. The easy-to-make cups are delectable dishes for our creamy peppermint ice cream that's made by enhancing vanilla ice cream with crushed candies. High in taste but low in fat,* Strawberry-Orange Frozen Yogurt *can be whipped up using flavored gelatin, yogurt, and strawberries.*

CHOCOLATE PEPPERMINT CUPS

- 1 package (9 ounces) round peppermint candies
- 1 quart vanilla ice cream, softened
- 1/2 cup plus 1 heaping tablespoon semisweet chocolate chips
- 4 ounces chocolate candy coating
- 10 aluminum foil muffin cups

Place candies in a resealable plastic bag and coarsely crush; reserve 1/4 cup for garnish. Finely crush remaining candies and combine with ice cream in a medium bowl. Cover and place in freezer.

Combine chocolate chips and candy coating in the top of a double boiler over simmering water until chocolate mixture melts. Invert foil cups onto a baking sheet.

Spoon chocolate mixture into a pastry bag fitted with a small round tip (#4). Randomly pipe chocolate onto foil cups. Place pan in freezer until chocolate hardens.

To serve, carefully remove foil cups from chocolate. Spoon ice cream into chocolate cups; garnish with reserved crushed candies.

Yield: 10 servings

STRAWBERRY-ORANGE FROZEN YOGURT

- 1 cup boiling water
- 1 package (3 ounces) orange gelatin
- 2 containers (8 ounces each) strawberry low-fat yogurt
- 1 cup chopped fresh or frozen strawberries

    Fresh whole strawberries to garnish

In a medium bowl, stir boiling water into gelatin until gelatin dissolves. Process gelatin mixture, yogurt, and strawberries in a food processor until smooth. Pour into a large bowl, cover, and freeze 3 hours or until firm. Break up mixture with a spoon; beat with an electric mixer until smooth. Cover and freeze until firm. Remove from freezer 10 minutes before serving. Garnish with strawberries.

Yield: about 1 quart frozen yogurt

As simple as it is luscious, Ice Cream Sundae Cake is created with alternating layers of pound cake and fruity ice cream. This scrumptious masterpiece will impress even your most discriminating guests.

ICE CREAM SUNDAE CAKE

1 package (16 ounces) pound
   cake mix
²/₃ cup water
2 eggs
1 quart vanilla ice cream, softened
1 container (11.75 ounces)
   strawberry ice cream topping
1 can (8 ounces) crushed pineapple,
   drained
¼ cup chopped pecans
2 jars (6 ounces each) maraschino
   cherries
1 container (12 ounces) non-dairy
   whipped topping, thawed

Chocolate sprinkles and whole
   maraschino cherries to garnish

Preheat oven to 325 degrees. Combine cake mix, water, and eggs in a large bowl; beat at low speed of an electric mixer 30 seconds. Beat at medium speed 2 minutes. Pour into 3 greased 8-inch round cake pans. Bake 18 to 23 minutes or until a toothpick inserted in center of cake comes out clean. Cool in pans 5 minutes. Remove from pans and cool completely on a wire rack.

In a large bowl, combine ice cream, strawberry topping, pineapple, and pecans.

Line two 8-inch round cake pans with plastic wrap. Spread ice cream mixture into prepared pans. Cover and freeze until firm.

Place 1 cake layer on a serving plate. Top with 1 ice cream layer. Repeat with remaining cake and ice cream layers. Freeze until ready to serve.

To serve, process maraschino cherries in a food processor until coarsely chopped; drain. In a medium bowl, fold cherry pieces into whipped topping. Spread mixture over top and sides of cake. Garnish with chocolate sprinkles and whole cherries.

Yield: about 12 servings

TOP IT OFF!

Turn plain desserts into fabulous flavor pleasers with our selection of quick-and-easy sauces. Ideal for occasions when time is short, these recipes require only a few simple ingredients, most of which you probably already have in your pantry. Store-bought jellies, jams, and ice cream toppings help you get a fast start on many of these accompaniments. Served with cake, fresh fruit, ice cream, and more, the tempting toppers make the ordinary extraordinary!

Honey-Blueberry Topping	Butter-Pecan Sauce
Toffee Sauce	Hot Apple Spice Sundae Sauce
Walnut-Raisin Sauce	Peanut Butter Sauce
Peaches and Cream Sauce	Chocolate Fudge Sauce
Quick Berry Sauce	Gingersnap Sauce
Pineapple-Ginger Sauce	Apricot-Orange Curd
Creamy Caramel-Nut Sauce	Orange Crème Chantilly
Citrus Fruit Fondue	Strawberry-Lemon Sauce
Caribbean Banana Sauce	Cherry-Walnut Sauce

Kissed with a hint of brandy, Honey-Blueberry Topping (left) *turns plain breakfast waffles into something special. T* *fast-to-make sauce also dresses up ice cream or cake in an instant. Chocolate-covered candy bits are stirred into butte Toffee Sauce for a pleasing crunch.*

HONEY-BLUEBERRY TOPPING

    1 jar (16 ounces) honey
    1 cup frozen blueberries, thawed
 1/4 cup finely chopped walnuts
    2 tablespoons brandy
       Waffles, ice cream, or cake to
         serve

Combine all ingredients in a medium bowl. Serve at room temperature over waffles, ice cream, or cake. Store in an airtight container in refrigerator.

Yield: about 2 cups sauce

TOFFEE SAUCE

1 1/2 cups sugar
    1 cup evaporated milk
 1/4 cup butter or margarine
 1/4 cup light corn syrup
       Dash of salt
    1 package (6 ounces) chocolate-
         covered toffee bits

       Cake or ice cream to serve

In a heavy medium saucepan, combine sugar, evaporated milk, butter, corn syrup, and salt. Stirring constantly, cook over medium heat until butter melts. Increase

heat to medium-high and bring to a boil; boil 1 minute. Remove from heat and coo 15 minutes. Stir in toffee bits. Serve warm over cake or ice cream. Store in an airtigl container in refrigerator.

Yield: about 3 cups sauce

92

WALNUT-RAISIN SAUCE

1/2 tablespoons cornstarch
1/4 cup water
1 cup raisins
1/2 cup granulated sugar
1/2 cup firmly packed brown sugar
1/8 teaspoon salt
1/2 cups apple cider
1 tablespoon butter or margarine
1 tablespoon apple cider vinegar
1 cup chopped walnuts
   Ice cream or pudding to serve

Dissolve cornstarch in water in a small
bowl. In a heavy medium saucepan,
combine raisins, sugars, and salt. Add cider,
butter, and vinegar. Stirring frequently,
bring to a boil over medium heat. Stir in
cornstarch mixture until sauce begins to
thicken. Stir in walnuts; cook about
minutes. Remove from heat. Serve warm
sauce over ice cream or pudding. Store in
an airtight container in refrigerator.

Yield: about 2 2/3 cups sauce

PEACHES AND CREAM SAUCE

1/2 cup peach preserves
1 teaspoon lemon juice
1/2 cups sour cream
2 tablespoons firmly packed
      brown sugar
1/2 teaspoon apple pie spice

   Fresh fruit, cake, or custard
      to serve

Combine peach preserves and lemon
juice in a medium bowl. Stir in sour cream,
brown sugar, and apple pie spice until well
blended. Chill 1 hour to allow flavors to
blend. Serve over fruit, cake, or custard.
Store in an airtight container.

Yield: about 2 cups sauce

A dreamy dessert topping, Walnut-Raisin Sauce (top) *blends nuts and fruit in an apple cider base. Peach preserves, lemon juice, and sour cream are combined to make luscious Peaches and Cream Sauce. Touched with apple pie spice, it's a lovely complement to fresh fruit, cake, or custard.*

QUICK BERRY SAUCE

  2 tablespoons cornstarch
$^1\!/_4$ cup water
  1 jar (12 ounces) raspberry jelly
  1 package (10 ounces) frozen
       sweetened sliced strawberries,
       thawed
$^1\!/_2$ cup sugar

    Pudding, cake, or ice cream to
    serve

In a small bowl, dissolve cornstarch in
water. Combine jelly, strawberries, and
sugar in a medium saucepan over medium
high heat; stir until jelly melts. Stir
cornstarch mixture into fruit mixture.
Stirring constantly, boil about 10 minutes
until mixture thickens. Serve sauce warm
cold over pudding, cake, or ice cream.
Store in an airtight container in refrigerate

Yield: about $2^3\!/_4$ cups sauce

PINEAPPLE-GINGER SAUCE

$^3\!/_4$ cup firmly packed brown sugar
  2 tablespoons cornstarch
  1 can (20 ounces) crushed
       pineapple in heavy syrup
  2 teaspoons finely chopped
       crystallized ginger

    Pie, cake, or ice cream to serve

Combine brown sugar and cornstarch i
a small bowl. Heat undrained pineapple
and ginger in a medium saucepan over
medium heat 5 minutes. Stirring constantl
add brown sugar mixture; cook 5 to
7 minutes or until mixture thickens. Serve
warm over pie, cake, or ice cream. Store
in an airtight container in refrigerator.

Yield: about $2^1\!/_2$ cups sauce

These tasty toppings can be made in minutes! Try Quick Berry Sauce (top)
over pudding, cake, or ice cream. It's easy to make with raspberry jelly and
frozen strawberries. The aromatic flavor of ginger is especially inviting in
Pineapple-Ginger Sauce, a fruit-packed indulgence that's best served warm.

Three simple ingredients are all it takes to stir up Creamy Caramel-Nut Sauce (left). Lemon and orange juices and ...ts add lively flavor to Citrus Fruit Fondue, a tangy dip that's wonderful served with fresh fruit.

...EAMY CARAMEL-NUT SAUCE

1   container (12.5 ounces) caramel
       ice cream topping
1   jar (7 ounces) marshmallow
       creme
1   cup chopped pecans
       Cake or ice cream to serve

...ombine caramel topping, marshmallow
...me, and pecans in a large saucepan over
...dium-low heat. Stirring frequently, cook
...ut 4 minutes or until mixture is well
...nded. Serve warm over cake or ice
...am. Store in an airtight container in
...igerator.

...ld: about 2³/₄ cups sauce

CITRUS FRUIT FONDUE

1   cup sugar
2   tablespoons all-purpose flour
1   cup boiling water
¹/₄   cup butter or margarine
1   tablespoon lemon juice
1   tablespoon orange juice
¹/₄   teaspoon grated lemon zest
¹/₄   teaspoon grated orange zest
¹/₈   teaspoon ground ginger
       Orange zest strips to garnish
       Fresh fruit slices to serve

   Combine sugar and flour in a heavy
medium saucepan. Whisking constantly over
medium-high heat, add boiling water. Bring

mixture to a boil; add butter and cook
about 3 minutes or until mixture thickens.
Remove from heat and whisk in juices,
grated zests, and ginger. Garnish with
orange zest strips. Serve with fruit slices.
Store in an airtight container in refrigerator.

Yield: about 1³/₄ cups sauce

A warm tropical pleaser, Caribbean Banana Sauce (left) *is laced with dark rum and packed with sliced bananas. Wa* up ordinary desserts with rich Butter-Pecan Sauce, a quick-to-make topping that's studded with nuts.

CARIBBEAN BANANA SAUCE

  1 cup firmly packed brown sugar
1½ tablespoons cornstarch
  1 cup water
¼ cup butter or margarine
¼ cup dark rum
  3 bananas, sliced

    Crepes, cake, or ice cream to serve

Combine brown sugar and cornstarch in a heavy medium saucepan. Stirring constantly over medium-high heat, gradually add water. Bring mixture to a boil; cook 3 minutes or until mixture begins to thicken. Add butter; stir until butter melts. Remove from heat. Stir in rum and banana slices. Serve warm over crepes, cake, or ice cream. Store in an airtight container in refrigerator.

Yield: about 2²/₃ cups sauce

BUTTER-PECAN SAUCE

½ cup sugar
  1 tablespoon cornstarch
  1 cup boiling water
½ cup chopped pecans
  1 tablespoon butter
    Dash of salt
  1 teaspoon vanilla-butter-nut flavoring

    Ice cream or cake to serve

Combine sugar and cornstarch in a heavy medium saucepan. Stirring constantly over medium heat, gradually add boiling water. Add pecans, butter, and salt; cook about 4 minutes or until mixture thickens. Remove from heat. Stir in vanilla-butter-nut flavoring. Serve warm over ice cream or cake. Store in an airtight container in refrigerator.

Yield: about 1¼ cups sauce

HOT APPLE SPICE SUNDAE SAU

  2 tablespoons butter or margarine
  2 tablespoons firmly packed brown sugar
½ teaspoon ground cinnamon
  1 can (21 ounces) apple pie filling
¼ cup chopped walnuts

    Ice cream to serve

Combine butter, brown sugar, and cinnamon in a medium saucepan. Stirring frequently, cook over medium-low heat until butter melts. Add pie filling and increase heat to medium-high. Continue stir frequently until mixture comes to a b Remove from heat and stir in walnuts. Se warm over ice cream. Store in an airtight container in refrigerator.

Yield: about 2¼ cups sauce

...NUT BUTTER SAUCE

    ...cup firmly packed brown sugar
    ...cup whipping cream
    ...cup crunchy peanut butter
    ...teaspoon vanilla extract
    Ice cream or cake to serve

...ombine brown sugar and whipping
...m in a medium microwave-safe bowl;
...k until smooth. Add peanut butter
...microwave on high power (100%)
...nutes; whisk until melted. Stir in
...lla. Serve warm over ice cream or cake.
...e in an airtight container in refrigerator.

...d: about 2 cups sauce

...OCOLATE FUDGE SAUCE

    ...cans (5 ounces each) evaporated
        milk
    ...package (6 ounces) semisweet
        chocolate chips
    ...cup butter or margarine
    ...cups sifted confectioners sugar
    ...teaspoon vanilla extract
    Ice cream or cake to serve

...a large microwave-safe bowl, combine
...orated milk, chocolate chips, and
...er; cover with plastic wrap. Microwave
...igh power (100%) 5 minutes; carefully
...ove plastic wrap and stir until smooth.
...confectioners sugar; stir until well
...ded. Microwave uncovered on high
...er (100%) 6 minutes, stirring every
...inutes. Stir in vanilla. Serve warm over
...cream or cake. Store in an airtight
...tainer in refrigerator.

...d: about 2²/₃ cups sauce

*Turn simple desserts into sumptuous fare with these extra-easy delights.
(Clockwise from top) Peanut Butter Sauce blends a favorite childhood staple
with brown sugar and cream. Canned pie filling gives you a head start on
making Hot Apple Spice Sundae Sauce. Always a hit, our Chocolate Fudge Sauce
is fast to fix in the microwave.*

GINGERSNAP SAUCE

- 12 gingersnap cookies (2-inch diameter)
- 1 container (12.5 ounces) caramel ice cream topping
- 3 tablespoons firmly packed brown sugar
- 1/4 cup chopped pecans

  Ice cream or cake to serve

Place cookies in a resealable plastic b Use a rolling pin to finely crush cookies. Combine cookie crumbs, caramel toppir and brown sugar in a small saucepan. Stirring frequently, cook over medium h about 5 minutes or until sugar dissolves. Stir in pecans. Serve warm over ice crea or cake. Store in an airtight container in refrigerator.

Yield: about 1 1/2 cups sauce

APRICOT-ORANGE CURD

- 1 cup unsalted butter or margarine
- 3/4 cup sugar
- 4 eggs
- 1/2 cup apricot nectar
- 1/3 cup frozen orange juice concentrate, thawed

  Cake to serve

Place butter in a small microwave-saf bowl. Microwave on high power (100%) 1 minute or until butter melts. Combine sugar, eggs, apricot nectar, and juice concentrate in a medium microwave-saf bowl; beat until well blended. Stir in mel butter. Microwave on high power (100% 5 to 7 minutes or until mixture thickens coats the back of a spoon, whisking after each minute. Serve warm over cake. Stor in an airtight container in refrigerator.

Yield: about 3 cups sauce

Just as the name suggests, Gingersnap Sauce (top) has the goodness of a favorite cookie blended right in! Prepared in the microwave, Apricot-Orange Curd is made with apricot nectar and frozen orange juice concentrate.

Reward your taste buds with these yummy creations! (From left) *Orange Crème Chantilly is a lightly sweetened
whipped topping that's flavored with honey, vanilla, and orange liqueur. Strawberry-Lemon Sauce is a no-hassle
combination of strawberry jam and frozen lemonade. Cherry-Walnut Sauce can be stirred up in a jiffy using cherry
* and dried cherries.*

ORANGE CRÈME CHANTILLY

1 cup whipping cream
2 tablespoons honey
1 teaspoon sugar
2 tablespoons orange-flavored
   liqueur
1 teaspoon vanilla extract
   Pudding, ice cream, cake, or fresh
     fruit to serve

Whisk whipping cream, honey, and
sugar in a chilled bowl just until soft peaks
form. Fold in liqueur and vanilla. Serve
immediately over pudding, ice cream,
cake, or fruit.

Yield: about 2¹/₃ cups sauce

STRAWBERRY-LEMON SAUCE

1 jar (18 ounces) strawberry jam
1 container (6 ounces) frozen
   lemonade concentrate, thawed
2 tablespoons light corn syrup
   Pudding, fresh fruit, or cake
     to serve

Whisk jam, lemonade concentrate, and
corn syrup in a small bowl. Serve over
pudding, fruit, or cake. Store in an airtight
container in refrigerator.

Yield: about 2¹/₂ cups sauce

CHERRY-WALNUT SAUCE

1 jar (10 ounces) cherry jelly
¹/₂ cup dried cherries (available at
   gourmet food stores)
2 tablespoons lemon juice
¹/₂ cup chopped toasted walnuts
   Pie, ice cream, or cake to serve

Combine jelly, dried cherries, and lemon
juice in a heavy small saucepan over
medium-low heat. Stirring occasionally,
cover and cook 5 minutes or until jelly
melts. Stir in walnuts. Serve warm over pie,
ice cream, or cake. Store in an airtight
container in refrigerator.

Yield: about 1¹/₄ cups sauce

SPEEDY KID PLEASERS

Children have three very simple requests when it comes to dessert — make it fast, make it fun, and make it taste good! Luckily, we've come up with lots of speedy kid pleasers to fill their orders. Most of our treats can be prepared in less than thirty minutes using store-bought items like cookies, refrigerated doughs, ice cream, and candy decorations. Best of all, youngsters can help make or decorate many of these simple, child-friendly goodies. For birthdays, sleep-overs, or any occasion that calls for snacks in a hurry, turn to this clever collection!

UPSIDE-DOWN CLOWN CONES

   1 container (16 ounces) vanilla
        ready-to-spread frosting
   6 sugar ice-cream cones
        Sprinkles
        Small gumdrops
   6 large scalloped-edged cookies
        (about 3-inch diameter)
   6 large scoops vanilla ice cream,
        firmly frozen
        Orange jelly beans
        Chocolate chips
        Red jelly beans
        Red string licorice

Spread frosting on wide end of cones;
roll in sprinkles. Press 1 gumdrop on po
of each cone. Place 1 cookie on each of
6 serving plates. Place 1 scoop ice cream
each cookie and invert cones on top of ic
cream. Working quickly, press orange je
beans on sides of ice cream for hair. Pre
chocolate chips on ice cream for eyes. Cu
3 red jelly beans in half and press on ice
cream for noses. Cut small pieces of lico
and press on ice cream for mouths. Plac
freezer until ready to serve.

Yield: 6 servings

KITE CAKE

   1 package (18.25 ounces)
        chocolate cake mix with
        pudding in the mix
1¼ cups water
   3 eggs
⅓ cup vegetable oil
   1 container (16 ounces) white
        chocolate ready-to-spread
        frosting
        Yellow, blue, and red paste food
        coloring
        Jelly beans, red string licorice,
        and bow-tie pasta to decorate

Make a birthday celebration especially memorable with Upside-Down Clown Cones! These smiley-face delights are simple — and fun — to make using cookies, candies, and purchased frosting to dress up ice cream and sugar cones.

This whimsical Kite Cake is a breeze to put together! Prepared with chocolate cake mix, its high-flying shape is ~ated by cutting the baked cake diagonally, turning one half over, and matching the cut edges. The cake is topped ~th colorfully tinted ready-to-spread frosting and jelly beans, then finished with a licorice tail and pasta "ties."

~reheat oven to 350 degrees. In a large
~wl, combine cake mix, water, eggs and
~. Beat at low speed of an electric mixer
~ seconds. Beat at medium speed
~inutes. Pour batter into a greased and
~ured 9 x 13-inch baking pan. Bake 28 to
~ minutes or until a toothpick inserted in
~ter of cake comes out clean. Cool in pan

15 minutes. Remove from pan and cool
completely on a wire rack.

Make a diagonal cut across cake from
1 corner to the opposite corner. Turn 1 cut
piece of cake over, matching cut edges.
Transfer to a serving dish. Tint 1/2 cup
frosting yellow, 1/2 cup blue, and 1/3 cup
red; leave remainder white. Reserve a small

amount of red frosting to attach pasta. Use a
small knife to score a very light line across
top of cake, connecting points of kite. Frost
top and sides of cake as shown in photo.
Decorate with jelly beans. Arrange licorice
for tail. Use reserved frosting to attach pasta
to licorice.

Yield: about 20 servings

103

These seaside surprises will add tropical flair to a pool party! Yummy candy fish splish splash in our Go Fish Pudding "ponds" (left). Sure to reel in squeals of delight, they're fast to make with gelatin and whipped topping. Served warm, Banana Boats are packed with a cargo of chocolate and peanut butter chips, marshmallows, and jam.

GO FISH PUDDING

  1 cup boiling water
  1 package (3 ounces) blue gelatin
  1 cup cold water
  1 container (8 ounces) frozen non-
      dairy whipped topping, thawed
    Gummi fish to decorate

In a medium bowl, stir boiling water into gelatin until gelatin dissolves. Stir in cold water. Refrigerate about 1½ hours or until partially set. Fold in whipped topping.

Spoon into serving bowls and refrigerate 30 minutes. To serve, decorate with gummi fish.

Yield: about 6 servings

BANANA BOATS

  6 bananas
      Milk chocolate chips
      Miniature marshmallows
      Peanut butter chips
      Strawberry jam

Preheat oven to 400 degrees. For each banana, peel back 1 skin segment in cur[ve] of banana without removing peel. Using [a] small spoon, scoop out a small portion [of] banana along entire length. Place favorit[e] mixture of fillings in banana; replace pe[el.] Place bananas in an 8-inch square bakin[g] pan, propping ends of bananas on sides [of] pan. Bake 6 to 8 minutes or until fillings melt. For each banana, remove peel covering filling and 1 skin segment on ea[ch] side. Serve warm.

Yield: about 6 servings

CREAMY ORANGE CONES

...your party cups to freeze and serve ...es.

4 cups boiling water
1 package (3 ounces) orange gelatin
2 cups vanilla ice cream, softened
1 sugar ice-cream cones
  Whipped cream and sprinkles to decorate

...using paper cups to hold cones, cut ...inch circles in bottoms of eleven ...unce cups. Invert cups onto a jellyroll ...; set aside.

...n a medium bowl, stir boiling water into ...tin until gelatin dissolves. Allow mixture ...ool 5 minutes. Whisk in ice cream. Chill ...ture 20 minutes or until almost set. ...on into cones; place cones in inverted ...s. Freeze until firm. Decorate with ...pped cream and sprinkles. Serve ...ediately.

...d: 11 servings

CHOCOLATE-PEANUT BUTTER GORP SNACKS

8 cups round toasted oat cereal
2 cups raisins
1 cup dry-roasted peanuts
1 package (12 ounces) semisweet chocolate chips
1/2 cup smooth peanut butter

...n a large bowl, combine cereal, raisins, ...d peanuts. Place chocolate chips and ...nut butter in a medium saucepan. ...ring constantly, cook over low heat until ...colate melts and mixture is smooth. ...r chocolate mixture over cereal mixture; ... until well coated. Drop about ... tablespoonfuls of mixture into paper ...ffin cups or onto waxed paper. Use ...gers to press mixture together if ...essary. Allow chocolate to harden.

...ld: about 4 1/2 dozen snacks

Take a break from birthday cake and stir up these super-simple munchies! Topped with whipped cream and candy sprinkles, Creamy Orange Cones (top) are made by filling sugar cones with a smooth, tangy mixture of orange gelatin and vanilla ice cream. Chocolate-Peanut Butter Gorp Snacks are packed with toasted oat cereal, raisins, and peanuts.

Let our UFO's (Undeniably Fun Objects) touch down at your child's party and get ready for giggles that are out of this world! Plain purchased cookies are simply dipped in melted vanilla candy coating and decorated with pretzel sticks and candies to create Flying Saucer Cookies.

FLYING SAUCER COOKIES

  12 ounces vanilla candy coating, chopped
   1 dozen cookies (about 2½-inch diameter)
      Variety of candies
      Thin stick pretzels

Stirring constantly, melt candy coating a small saucepan over low heat. Place ea cookie on a fork and dip into candy coat until covered. Place cookies on a wire ra with waxed paper underneath. Decorate with candies and pretzels to resemble fly saucers; allow coating to harden.

Yield: 1 dozen cookies

PIRATE'S COOKIES IN A TREASURE CHEST

PIRATE'S COOKIES

   1 package (20 ounces) refrigerated sugar cookie dough, softened
  1½ cups finely crushed corn flake cereal
      Yellow paste food coloring

Combine cookie dough and cereal crumbs in a medium bowl; tint light yello Cover dough and refrigerate until well chilled.

Preheat oven to 350 degrees. Shape dough into ¾-inch balls. Place on a ligh greased baking sheet. Flatten balls slightl with fingers. Bake 8 to 10 minutes or unt bottoms are lightly browned. Transfer cookies to a wire rack to cool.

Yield: about 6½ dozen cookies

TREASURE CHEST

   5 chocolate graham crackers (about 2½ x 5 inches)
   1 tube (4.25 ounces) chocolate decorating icing with a set of decorating tips
   2 pretzel sticks, each cut 1½ inches long
      Gold dragées

Young swashbucklers won't have to dig for riches with our Pirate's Cookies in a Treasure Chest nearby! The crunchy den nuggets are made with tinted refrigerated cookie dough and crushed corn flakes. Holding a fortune in sweet prises, the chocolaty treasure box is assembled using graham crackers, pretzel sticks, and decorating icing and dded with gold dragées.

(Note: To assemble treasure chest, use a all round tip to pipe icing, holding each cker in place until icing sets.) Place racker (bottom of chest) on a flat face. Pipe icing along long edges of cker. Press 1 long edge of 2 crackers icing for front and back of chest g. 1).

. 1

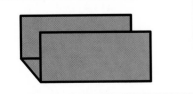

Cut 1 cracker in half to form 2 squares. Pipe icing along inside edges of each end of chest. Press each cracker square into icing for ends of chest as shown in Fig. 2.

Fig. 2

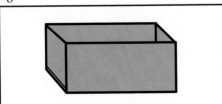

Pipe icing onto ends of pretzels pieces; set aside. Pipe icing along 1 long edge of remaining cracker (top of chest). Place on

long edge of back cracker, using pretzel pieces to prop top open about 2½ inches (Fig. 3).

Fig. 3

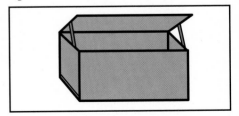

Use icing to attach dragées to chest. Allow icing to harden. Fill chest with Pirate's Cookies.

Yield: 1 treasure chest

107

CHINATOWN CEREAL SQUARES

5 cups bite-size square rice cereal
1 can (3 ounces) chow mein noodles
1 cup dry-roasted peanuts
1 package (10.5 ounces) miniature marshmallows
6 tablespoons butter or margarine
12 ounces vanilla candy coating, chopped

In a large bowl, combine cereal, chow mein noodles, and peanuts. In a large saucepan, combine marshmallows and butter. Cook over low heat until smooth, stirring frequently. Remove from heat and add candy coating; stir until smooth. Pour marshmallow mixture over cereal mixture; stir until well coated. Use greased hands to press mixture into a greased 9 x 13-inch baking dish. Cool completely. Cut into 2-inch squares.

Yield: about 2 dozen squares

PINEAPPLE CREAMSICLES

2 cups vanilla ice cream, softened
1 can (8 ounces) crushed pineapple in juice
7 paper cups (3-ounce size)
7 wooden craft sticks
Sprinkles to decorate

Combine ice cream and undrained pineapple. Spoon evenly into cups; insert craft stick into each cup. Freeze until firm. To serve, let stand at room temperature 10 minutes. Remove from cups; roll in sprinkles. Serve immediately.

Yield: 7 servings

Chinatown Cereal Squares (top) get their delicious crunch from a mixture of square rice cereal, chow mein noodles, and peanuts. For a cool and creamy treat, you'll want to make plenty of kid-size Pineapple Creamsicles! The fruity freezer pleasers feature crushed pineapple stirred into vanilla ice cream. Youngsters can roll them in candy sprinkles just before eating.

Deliver these taste-tempting tidbits along with your birthday greetings! Popcorn Cake S'Mores (top) begin with caramel corn cakes. The crispy snacks are topped with a peanut butter-marshmallow spread and sprinkled with miniature chocolate chips. Tinted a variety of colors, refrigerated sugar cookie dough is the only ingredient you'll need to fashion Rainbow Cookies.

POPCORN CAKE S'MORES

1/2 cup marshmallow creme
6 tablespoons smooth peanut butter
6 caramel corn cakes (about 4-inch diameter)
1/3 cup semisweet chocolate mini chips

In a small bowl, stir marshmallow creme and peanut butter with a wooden spoon until well blended. Spread on top of caramel corn cakes. Sprinkle chocolate chips over cakes, lightly pressing chips into topping.

Yield: 6 servings

RAINBOW COOKIES

1 package (20 ounces) refrigerated sugar cookie dough
Red, yellow, green, and blue paste food coloring

Divide cookie dough into 4 equal portions. Tint each portion of dough a different color (blend color into dough by kneading or by cutting in with a fork). Between sheets of plastic wrap, shape each piece of dough into a 4 x 8 x 1/4-inch rectangle. Remove plastic wrap. Stack red, yellow, green, and blue rectangles of dough on top of each other. Cover with plastic wrap and freeze 1 hour or until firm.

Preheat oven to 375 degrees. Returning dough to freezer between batches, cut dough into 1/4-inch-thick slices and place on a lightly greased baking sheet. Curve cookies to resemble rainbows. Bake 5 to 7 minutes or until edges begin to brown (do not overbake). Transfer to a wire rack to cool completely.

Yield: about 2 1/2 dozen cookies

STRAWBERRY-CREAM CHEESE SNAILS

- 3 tablespoons granulated sugar
- 1 teaspoon ground cinnamon
- 8 slices thin-sliced white bread
- 1/2 cup strawberry-flavored cream cheese
- 4 tablespoons butter or margarine, melted

Preheat oven to 350 degrees. Combine sugar and cinnamon in a small bowl; sprinkle on waxed paper. Trim crusts from 3 sides of bread. Lightly flatten bread with a rolling pin. Evenly spread about 1 tablespoon cream cheese on each slice bread. Beginning at edge opposite crust, roll up bread. Brush with melted butter a roll in sugar mixture. Cut each roll into 4 equal pieces. Place each piece, cut side up, on an ungreased baking sheet. Slightly pull crust edge away from each slice to resemble a snail's head. Bake 10 to 12 minutes or until lightly browned. Serve warm.

Yield: 32 snails

CONFETTI COOKIE POPS

- 1 package (20 ounces) refrigerated sugar cookie dough
- 18 craft sticks
- 12 ounces vanilla candy coating Blue powdered food coloring
  Sprinkles to decorate

Preheat oven to 350 degrees. Divide cookie dough into 18 equal pieces; shape each piece into a ball. Insert a craft stick into each ball. Place on a greased baking sheet; flatten into 2-inch circles. Bake 11 13 minutes or until edges are golden brown. Transfer cookies to a wire rack to cool.

Stirring constantly, melt candy coating in a large saucepan over low heat. Remove

Let the good times begin with these quick and tasty surprises! Cinnamony sweet, Strawberry-Cream Cheese Snails (top) won't be slow to disappear. The quick treats are fun to make with just a few simple ingredients. Confetti Cookie Pops are made by baking refrigerated dough on craft sticks. Tinted candy coating provides a pretty blue background for the whimsical colored sprinkles.

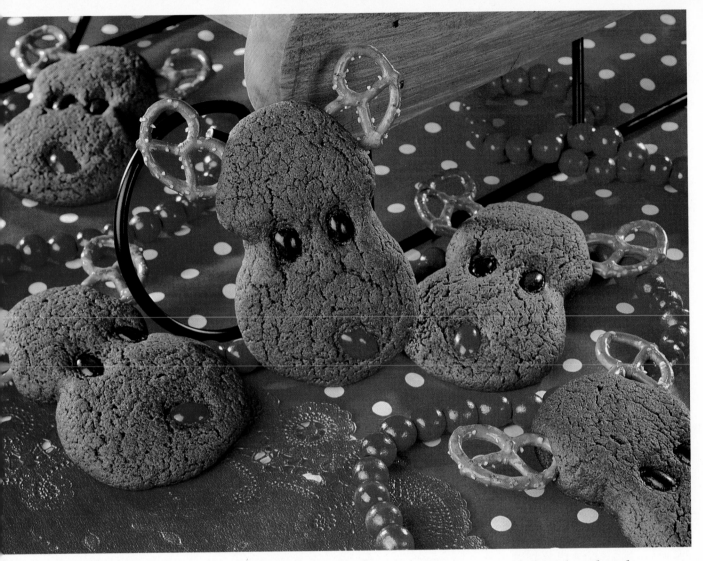

Our adorable Gingerbread Reindeer Cookies are ideal for a classroom Christmas party. Made with packaged gingerbread mix, the spicy treats have pretzel antlers and candy eyes and noses.

m heat; tint light blue. Dip tops of okies into coating. Place on waxed paper d decorate with sprinkles. Allow coating harden.

eld: 18 cookie pops

INGERBREAD REINDEER OOKIES

1 package (14 ounces) gingerbread mix

2 eggs
1/4 cup vegetable oil
Small pretzel twists
Brown and red jelly beans

Preheat oven to 350 degrees. In a large bowl, combine gingerbread mix, eggs, and oil; stir until a soft dough forms. For each cookie, place a 1 1/2-inch ball of dough on a greased baking sheet. Flatten balls into a 3-inch oval shape. Use fingers to press in sides of each cookie about one-third from

1 end of cookie to resemble reindeer face. Press pretzels into cookies for antlers. Press jelly beans into cookies for eyes and noses. Bake 9 to 11 minutes or until bottoms of cookies are firm. Transfer cookies to a wire rack to cool.

Yield: about 1 dozen cookies

No-Hassle Holiday Treats

By their very nature, holidays call for extra-special fare. With this creative collection, you can serve up great desserts that reflect the spirit of occasions all through the year, from Valentine's Day to Christmas. These treats are all deliciously easy — and quick — to prepare, so you'll have more time to enjoy the festivities. We've even included several treats that children can help create. Year after year, you'll be turning to these yummy confections to sweeten your family celebrations!

Santa's Sleigh	Carrot-Raisin Scones
Cranberry-Lemon Trifle	Strawberry-Banana Cake
Cranberry-Nut Balls	Peach-Almond Pastries
Frozen Amaretto Fruitcake	Patriotic Cake
Christmas Mincemeat Bars	Glowworms
Strawberry Heart Cakes	Praline Pumpkin Pie
Creamy Mint Fudge	Pumpkin Streusel Cake
Easter Basket Cupcakes	Cranberry-Orange Squares

113

SANTA'S SLEIGH

1 tube (4.25 ounces) white decorating icing with a set of decorating tips
5 graham crackers (about 2½ x 5 inches)
2 candy canes (about 6½ inches long)

Dragées and candies to decorate

(*Note:* To assemble sleigh, use a small round tip to pipe icing unless otherwise indicated in instructions; hold each cracker in place until icing sets.) Place 1 cracker (bottom of sleigh) on a flat surface. Pipe icing along long edges of cracker. Press 1 long edge of 2 crackers into icing for sides of sleigh (Fig. 1).

Fig. 1

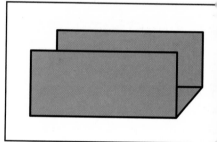

Pipe icing along inside edges of one end of sleigh. Press 1 cracker into icing for back of sleigh. (Fig. 2).

Fig. 2

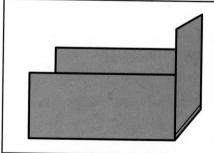

Cut 1 cracker in half to form 2 squares. Pipe icing along inside edges of remaining end of sleigh. Press 1 cracker half into icing for front of sleigh (Fig. 3).

Adorned with shiny dragées and colorful candies, these Santa's Sleigh cookies are easy to assemble using graham crackers and purchased decorating icing. Youngsters will enjoy creating the fun Christmas carriers, which are perfect for holding little bags of candy.

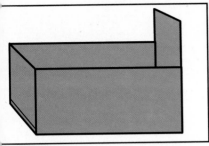

3

remaining cracker in half diagonally to
ke 2 triangles. Pipe icing along 2 uncut
ges of each triangle. Press pieces into
ck and side pieces of sleigh (Fig. 4).

4

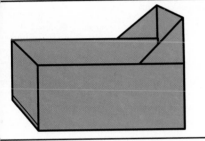

e a star tip to pipe icing along bottom
g edges of sleigh sides. Press candy
nes into icing. Decorate sleigh with
ditional icing, dragées, and candies.

eld: 1 sleigh

RANBERRY-LEMON TRIFLE

- 2 packages (4.4 ounces each)
    custard mix
- 5 cups milk
- 1 purchased pound cake loaf
    (16 ounces)
- 1/4 cup crème de cassis
- 1 jar (11 1/4 ounces) lemon curd
- 2 cans (16 ounces each) whole
    berry cranberry sauce

    Lemon slice and fresh cranberries
    to garnish

In a large saucepan, prepare custard mix
ith milk according to package directions.
over and chill about 30 minutes.

Adult palates will savor elegant Cranberry-Lemon Trifle (top), which layers crème de cassis-sprinkled pound cake with custard and cranberry sauce. Zesty Cranberry-Nut Balls will tickle your taste buds! The chewy no-bake candies are prepared with cranberry-orange relish, coconut, and pecans.

Cut pound cake into 1/4-inch slices. Place slices on a baking sheet. Sprinkle crème de cassis over slices. Fold lemon curd into custard. Place a layer of custard mixture in a 3 1/2-quart trifle bowl. Place a layer of cake over custard. Spoon a layer of cranberry sauce over cake. Repeat layers, ending with custard on top. Garnish with lemon slice and fresh cranberries. Cover and store in refrigerator.

Yield: about 18 servings

CRANBERRY-NUT BALLS

- 1 cup cranberry-orange relish
- 1 package (7 ounces) flaked
    coconut
- 1 cup finely chopped pecans
    Confectioners sugar

Combine cranberry-orange relish, coconut, and pecans in a medium bowl. Chill 2 hours. Shape into 1-inch balls (mixture will be sticky). Roll in confectioners sugar. Store in an airtight container in refrigerator.

Yield: about 3 1/2 dozen candies

Bursting with bits of fruit and pecans, Frozen Amaretto Fruitcake (left) stirs lots of traditional flavor into a frozen fantasy that begins with instant pudding and whipped topping. Delicious Christmas Mincemeat Bars have a crumbly crust made with oats and cake mix.

FROZEN AMARETTO FRUITCAKE

- 1 package (3.4 ounces) French vanilla instant pudding mix
- 2 cups milk
- 2 cups finely crushed amaretto cookies (about 1/2 of a 14.1-ounce tin)
- 1 cup chopped pecans
- 1 cup chopped dates
- 1 cup chopped green and red candied cherries
- 1 container (8 ounces) non-dairy whipped topping, thawed and divided
- 2 teaspoons amaretto
  Chopped green and red candied cherries to garnish

In a large bowl, add pudding mix to milk; beat until thickened. Fold in cookie crumbs, pecans, dates, 1 cup candied cherries, and half of whipped topping. Pour mixture into a lightly greased 7-inch springform pan. Cover and freeze overnight.

To serve, run a knife around sides of pan and remove sides. Fold amaretto into remaining whipped topping in a small bowl. Garnish each serving of fruitcake with flavored topping and candied cherries.

Yield: about 12 servings

CHRISTMAS MINCEMEAT BARS

- 1 package (18.25 ounces) yellow cake mix
- 2¹/₂ cups quick-cooking oats
- ³/₄ cup butter or margarine, melted
- 1 jar (27 ounces) mincemeat

Preheat oven to 375 degrees. In a medium bowl, combine cake mix, oats, and melted butter (mixture will be crumbly). Reserving 2 cups oat mixture, firmly press remaining mixture into bottom of a lightly greased 9 x 13-inch baking pan. Spread mincemeat over crust. Sprinkle reserved oat mixture over mincemeat. Bake 30 to 35 minutes or until topping is lightly browned. Cool in pan on a wire rack. Cut into 1 x 2-inch bars.

Yield: about 4 dozen bars

Share Valentine's Day sentiments with this irresistible confection! Individual Strawberry Heart Cakes are made with French vanilla cake mix and crowned with luscious fruit and a drizzling of candy coating.

STRAWBERRY HEART CAKES

1 package (18.25 ounces) French
    vanilla cake mix

⅓ cups water

3 eggs

⅓ cup vegetable oil

1 container (16 ounces) vanilla
    ready-to-spread frosting

2 packages (10 ounces each) frozen
    sweetened sliced strawberries,
    thawed

2 ounces vanilla candy coating,
    chopped

Preheat oven to 350 degrees. Grease and flour cups (3 inches wide) of a 6-mold heart-shaped baking pan. In a medium bowl, combine cake mix, water, eggs, and oil. Beat at low speed of an electric mixer 30 seconds. Beat at medium speed 2 minutes. Fill prepared cups about two-thirds full. Bake 15 to 18 minutes or until a toothpick inserted in center of cake comes out clean. Cool in pan 5 minutes. Remove from pan and cool completely on a wire rack.

Place cakes on individual serving plates. Frost sides of cakes. Spoon remaining frosting into a decorating bag fitted with a medium star tip. Pipe frosting around top edge of each cake. Spoon strawberries into center of each cake. Place candy coating in a small resealable plastic bag. Microwave on medium power (50%) about 2 minutes or until candy coating melts. Snip off 1 corner of bag; drizzle over strawberries. Serve immediately.

Yield: about 16 cakes

EASTER BASKET CUPCAKES

1¹/₃ cups flaked coconut
    Green liquid food coloring
1 package (18.25 ounces)
    chocolate fudge cake mix with
    pudding in the mix
1¹/₃ cups water
3 eggs
¹/₃ cup vegetable oil
2 containers (16 ounces each)
    vanilla ready-to-spread frosting
    Vanilla wafers, graham cereal
    squares, small jellybeans, and
    red string licorice to decorate

Preheat oven to 350 degrees. Place coconut in a small bowl; tint light green. a medium bowl, combine cake mix, wate eggs, and oil. Beat at low speed of an electric mixer 30 seconds. Beat at mediu speed 2 minutes. Fill greased and floured muffin cups about two-thirds full. Bake 18 to 23 minutes or until a toothpick inserted in center of cupcake comes out clean. Cool in pan 5 minutes. Remove fro pan and cool completely on a wire rack.

If necessary, use a serrated knife to lev tops of cupcakes. Frost sides and tops of cupcakes. Press vanilla wafers or cereal pieces onto sides of cupcakes. Sprinkle tinted coconut on tops of cupcakes. Press jellybeans into centers of cupcakes for eg Twist 2 pieces of licorice together to make each handle. Press a handle into each cupcake.

Yield: about 2 dozen cupcakes

The Irish aren't the only ones lucky enough to indulge in this St. Patrick's Day delight! Creamy Mint Fudge is created with white chocolate and sweetened condensed milk. A layer of chocolate tops each satiny bite.

CREAMY MINT FUDGE

2 packages (6 ounces each) white
    baking chocolate, chopped
¹/₂ cup sweetened condensed milk
1¹/₂ teaspoons vanilla extract
1 teaspoon mint extract
10 to 15 drops green food coloring
1 cup sifted confectioners sugar
¹/₂ cup semisweet chocolate chips

Combine white chocolate and sweetened condensed milk in a medium saucepan. Stirring constantly, cook over low heat until chocolate softens. Remove from heat; stir until chocolate melts. Stir in extracts, food coloring, and confectioners sugar. Spread into a greased 8-inch square baking pan. Chill 30 minutes or until firm.

Place chocolate chips in a small microwave-safe bowl. Microwave on high power (100%) 1 minute or until chocolate softens; stir until smooth. Spread over fudge. Chill 15 minutes or until chocolate hardens. Cut into 1-inch squares. Store in an airtight container in refrigerator.

Yield: about 3¹/₂ dozen pieces fudge

Kids will be "hoppy" to help make — and eat — Easter Basket Cupcakes (left)! *The whimsical chocolate treats are decorated with candies, cookies, cereal, and tinted coconut. Baking mix provides a head start on Carrot-Raisin Scones. Ideal for brunch, the biscuit-like pastries feature a pleasing blend of taste sensations.*

CARROT-RAISIN SCONES

2 cups buttermilk baking mix
1 tablespoon sugar
3/4 teaspoon dried orange peel
1/2 cup butter or margarine, chilled and cut into pieces
3/4 cup buttermilk
1/2 cup golden raisins
1/2 cup finely shredded carrot
2 tablespoons butter or margarine, melted

Preheat oven to 425 degrees. Combine baking mix, sugar, and orange peel in a medium bowl. Using a pastry blender or 2 knives, cut in chilled butter until mixture resembles coarse meal. Add buttermilk, raisins, and carrot, stirring with a fork just until moistened. Turn dough onto a lightly floured surface and knead 10 to 12 times. Pat dough into a 1/2-inch-thick rectangle. Use a 2 1/4 x 3 1/4-inch scalloped egg-shaped

cookie cutter to cut out scones. Place 2 inches apart on a lightly greased baking sheet. Bake 10 to 12 minutes or until tops are golden brown. Brush tops of scones with melted butter. Serve warm or transfer to a wire rack to cool completely.

Yield: about 1 dozen scones

Preheat oven to 350 degrees. Grease three 9-inch round cake pans and line bottoms with waxed paper. In a large bowl combine cake mix and gelatin. Add eggs, buttermilk, and oil; beat at low speed of a electric mixer 30 seconds. Beat at medium speed 2 minutes. Add 1 cup strawberries and mashed bananas to cake mixture; beat 1 minute or until well blended. Pour batter into prepared pans. Bake 25 to 30 minute or until a toothpick inserted in center of cake comes out clean. Cool in pans 15 minutes. Remove from pans and cool completely on a wire rack.

In a medium bowl, beat cream cheese, vanilla, and remaining 1/3 cup strawberries until fluffy. Gradually add confectioners sugar, beating until well blended. Spread icing between layers and on top and sides cake. Store in an airtight container in refrigerator. To serve, garnish with banan and strawberry slices and whole strawber

Yield: 12 to 14 servings

On Mother's Day, share a dreamy Strawberry-Banana Cake (bottom) flavored with fresh fruit and strawberry gelatin. The heavenly strawberry-cream cheese icing is inspirational! Delight Dad with Peach-Almond Pastries for Father's Day. Prepared with refrigerated pie crusts, these sugar-sprinkled pockets are filled with amaretto-laced peaches and toasted almonds.

STRAWBERRY-BANANA CAKE

1 package (18.25 ounces) white cake mix
1 package (3 ounces) strawberry gelatin
4 eggs
1 cup buttermilk
1/2 cup vegetable oil
1 1/3 cups sliced fresh strawberries, divided

1 cup mashed bananas (about 3 bananas)
1 package (8 ounces) cream cheese, softened
1 teaspoon vanilla extract
1 package (16 ounces) confectioners sugar

Banana and strawberry slices and whole strawberry to garnish

PEACH-ALMOND PASTRIES

1 can (21 ounces) peach pie filling
1/2 cup sliced almonds, toasted
2 tablespoons amaretto
1/2 teaspoon almond extract
1 package (15 ounces) refrigerated pie crusts, at room temperature
Vegetable cooking spray
2 tablespoons sugar
1/2 teaspoon ground cinnamon

Preheat oven to 425 degrees. Using a slotted spoon, remove peaches from pie filling (discard liquid) and place in a food processor. Add almonds, amaretto, and almond extract. Process until peaches are coarsely chopped; set aside.

Cut each pie crust into 8 triangles for a total of 16 triangles. Place 8 triangles on a baking sheet lightly sprayed with cooking spray. Spoon about 3 tablespoonfuls of

ch mixture into center of each triangle.
a heart-shaped aspic cutter to cut hearts
enters of remaining triangles. Place
out triangles over pie filling. Use a fork
crimp edges of dough together. Combine
ar and cinnamon in a small bowl. Lightly
ay tops of pastries with cooking spray;
inkle with sugar mixture. Bake 20 to
minutes or until tops are golden brown.
dges of crust brown too quickly, cover
h strips of aluminum foil. Serve warm.

ld: 8 servings

TRIOTIC CAKE

  1 package (18.25 ounces) French
      vanilla cake mix
 /3 cups water
  3 eggs
 /3 cup vegetable oil
  2 cups boiling water, divided
  1 package (3 ounces) strawberry
      gelatin
  1 package (3 ounces) blue gelatin
  1 container (8 ounces) frozen non-
      dairy whipped topping, thawed
      Blue and red decorating gel and
      small flags to decorate

Preheat oven to 350 degrees. Grease and
ur two 9-inch round cake pans. In a
dium bowl, combine cake mix, water,
gs, and oil. Beat at low speed of an
ctric mixer 30 seconds. Beat at medium
eed 2 minutes. Pour batter into prepared
ns. Bake 25 to 30 minutes or until a
thpick inserted in center of cake comes
t clean. Cool in pans 5 minutes. Remove
m pans and cool completely on a wire
ck.
  Place layers, top sides up, in 2 clean
inch round cake pans. Use a meat fork to
ke holes about 1½ inches apart in top of
ers. In separate bowls, stir 1 cup boiling
ter into each flavor of gelatin until gelatin
ssolves. Pour red gelatin mixture over

Our Patriotic Cake offers a fun salute to Independence Day! The star-spangled sweet gets its all-American flair from red and blue fruit-flavored gelatins, piped-on stars, and miniature flags.

1 layer. Pour blue gelatin mixture over other layer. Cover and chill 3 hours.

  Dip 1 cake pan into warm water about 10 seconds; unmold onto a serving plate, top side up. Spread about ¾ cup whipped topping over top. Unmold second cake layer; carefully place, top side up, on first layer. Spread top and sides of cake with remaining whipped topping. Pipe red and blue decorating gel stars on top of cake. Place flags in center of cake. Serve immediately.

Yield: about 16 servings

Colorful sugar crystals, licorice, and your child's imagination give Glowworms their Halloween gleam. Created with refrigerated cookie dough, the creepy crawlers are a "scream" come true!

GLOWWORMS

    Red string licorice
1   package (20 ounces) refrigerated
        sugar cookie dough
    Colored sugar crystals

Preheat oven to 350 degrees. Cut licorice into ½-inch-long pieces; set aside. Working with one-fourth of cookie dough at a time and keeping remainder in refrigerator, cut each fourth of dough into 12 pieces. Roll in sugar crystals, shaping into 4-inch-long pencil-size ropes. Place ropes on a lightly greased baking sheet; shape to resemble worms. Bake 6 to 8 minutes or until edges are golden brown. Press 2 pieces licorice into 1 end of each warm cookie for antennae. Transfer cookies to a wire rack to cool.

Yield: about 4 dozen cookies

PRALINE PUMPKIN PIE

1   purchased frozen pumpkin pie
        (1 pound, 10 ounces)
¼   cup butter or margarine
⅓   cup firmly packed brown sugar
2   tablespoons whipping cream
⅓   cup finely chopped pecans
½   teaspoon maple flavoring

Bake pumpkin pie according to package directions. Remove from oven while preparing topping.

Reduce heat to 350 degrees. In a small saucepan, melt butter over medium-high heat. Stir in brown sugar and cream. Bring to a boil, stirring constantly. Remove from heat; stir in pecans and maple flavoring. Pour mixture over hot pie. Bake 5 to 7 minutes or until topping bubbles. Cool to

room temperature before serving. Store an airtight container in refrigerator.

Yield: about 8 servings

PUMPKIN STREUSEL CAKE

STREUSEL

½   cup firmly packed brown sugar
½   cup finely chopped walnuts
1   tablespoon all-purpose flour
1   tablespoon butter or margarine,
        melted
1   teaspoon ground cinnamon

CAKE

1   package (18.25 ounces) spice
        cake mix
1   package (3.4 ounces) vanilla
        instant pudding mix
1   cup canned pumpkin
3   eggs
½   cup vegetable oil
½   cup water
1   teaspoon vanilla extract
    Confectioners sugar to garnish

For streusel, combine brown sugar, walnuts, flour, melted butter, and cinnamon in a small bowl.

Preheat oven to 350 degrees. For cake, combine cake mix, pudding mix, pumpkin, eggs, oil, water, and vanilla in a large bowl. Beat at low speed of an electric mixer 30 seconds. Beat at medium speed 2 minutes. Pour half of batter into a greased 10-inch springform pan with fluted tube insert or a 10-inch fluted tube pan; sprinkle streusel mixture over batter. Pour remaining batter into pan. Bake 35 to 42 minutes or until a toothpick inserted in cake comes out clean. Cool in pan 10 minutes. Remove sides of pan and invert onto a serving plate; cool completely. Sift confectioners sugar over cake to garnish.

Yield: about 16 servings

You'll give thanks for these holiday tempters! (From left) *Creamy Praline Pumpkin Pie is simply a purchased pie* ~~h~~anced *with an irresistible brown sugar-pecan topping.* Tangy Cranberry-Orange Squares *are prepared with cake* ~~mi~~x, *orange marmalade, and cranberry sauce for a refreshing approach to Thanksgiving dessert. Dusted with powdery* ~~sug~~ar, *Pumpkin Streusel Cake starts with cake and pudding mixes and has a cinnamon-walnut mixture baked inside.*

~~CR~~ANBERRY-ORANGE SQUARES

1 package (18.25 ounces) yellow
    cake mix
1 cup old-fashioned oats
$^1/_2$ teaspoon ground cinnamon
$^1/_4$ cup butter or margarine, softened
1 can (16 ounces) whole berry
    cranberry sauce
1 cup orange marmalade
1 cup chopped walnuts

Preheat oven to 350 degrees. In a large bowl, combine cake mix, oats, and cinnamon. Using a pastry blender or 2 knives, cut in butter until mixture is crumbly. Reserving $^1/_2$ cup oat mixture, firmly press remaining mixture into bottom of a greased $10^1/_2$ x $15^1/_2$-inch jellyroll pan. In a small bowl, combine cranberry sauce and marmalade. Spread evenly over crust.

Combine reserved oat mixture and walnuts. Sprinkle evenly over cranberry mixture; press lightly. Bake 35 to 40 minutes or until golden brown. Cool in pan on a wire rack. Cut into 2-inch squares.

Yield: about 35 squares

KITCHEN TIPS

MEASURING INGREDIENTS

Liquid measuring cups have a rim above the measuring line to keep liquid ingredients from spilling. Nested measuring cups are used to measure dry ingredients, butter, shortening, and peanut butter. Measuring spoons are used for measuring both dry and liquid ingredients.

To measure flour or granulated sugar: Spoon ingredient into nested measuring cup and level off with a knife. Do not pack down with spoon.

To measure confectioners sugar: Sift sugar, spoon lightly into nested measuring cup, and level off with a knife.

To measure brown sugar: Pack sugar into nested measuring cup and level off with a knife. Sugar should hold its shape when removed from cup.

To measure dry ingredients equaling less than 1/4 cup: Dip measuring spoon into ingredient and level off with a knife.

To measure butter, shortening, or peanut butter: Pack ingredient firmly into nested measuring cup and level off with a knife.

To measure liquids: Use a liquid measuring cup placed on a flat surface. Pour ingredient into cup and check measuring line at eye level.

To measure honey or syrup: For a more accurate measurement, lightly spray measuring cup or spoon with cooking spray before measuring so the liquid will release easily from cup or spoon.

TOASTING NUTS

To toast nuts, spread nuts on an ungreased baking sheet. Stirring occasionally, bake in a 350-degree oven 8 to 10 minutes or until nuts are slightly darker in color.

WHIPPING CREAM

For greatest volume, chill a glass bowl, beaters, and cream until well chilled before whipping. In warm weather, place chilled bowl over ice while whipping cream.

USING CHOCOLATE

Chocolate is best stored in a cool, dry place. Since it has a high cocoa butter content, chocolate may develop a grey film, or "bloom," when temperatures change. This grey film does not affect the taste.

When melting chocolate, a low temperature is important to prevent overheating and scorching that will affect flavor and texture. The following are methods for melting chocolate:

Chocolate can be melted in a heavy saucepan over low heat and stirred constantly until melted.

Melting chocolate in the top of a double boiler over hot, not boiling, water is a good method to prevent chocolate from overheating.

Using a microwave oven to melt chocolate is fast and convenient. Microwave chocolate in a microwave-safe container on medium-high power (80%) 1 minute; stir with a dry spoon. Continue to microwave as needed, stirring chocolate every 15 seconds until smooth. Frequent stirring is important, as the chocolate will appear not to be melting, but will be soft when stirred. A shiny appearance is another sign that chocolate is melting.

MAKING CHOCOLATE CURLS

Making chocolate curls for garnishes is not difficult, but it does take a little practice. The chocolate should be the correct firmness to form the curls, neither too soft nor too hard. Different types of baking chocolates may be used, but the most common ones are semisweet and unsweetened. They are packaged in boxes containing 1-ounce squares.

There are several methods for making chocolate curls. To make small, short curls, hold a baking chocolate square in your hand for a few minutes to slightly soften chocolate. Rub chocolate over shredding side (large holes) of a grater to form curls. For medium-size curls, use a vegetable peeler or chocolate curler (available in kitchen specialty shops) to shave the wide side (for wide curls) or thin side (for thin curls) of a chocolate square.

To make long, thin, loosely formed curls, melt 6 chocolate squares and pour into a foil-lined 3 1/4 x 5 1/4-inch loaf pan. Chill until chocolate is set (about 2 hours). Remove from pan and remove foil. Rub chocolate over shredding side (large holes) of a grater to form curls.

To make large curls, melt about 5 chocolate squares and pour into a jelly pan or onto a cookie sheet. Spread chocolate over pan. Chill about 10 minutes. Scrape across surface of chocolate with a long metal spatula, knife, teaspoon, or chocolate curler to form curls. The spatula and knife will form long, thin curls and the teaspoon and curler will form shorter curls. Return pan to refrigerator if chocolate becomes too soft. Use a toothpick to pick up curls.

MELTING CANDY COATING

To melt candy coating, place in the top of a double boiler over hot, not boiling, water, or in a heavy saucepan over low heat. Stir occasionally with a dry spoon until coating melts. Remove from heat and use for dipping as desired. To flavor candy coating, add a small amount of flavored oil. To thin coating, add a small amount of vegetable oil, but no water. If necessary, coating may be returned to heat to remelt.

PARING CITRUS FRUIT ZEST

o remove the zest or outer portion of
. (colored part) from citrus fruits, use a
grater or fruit zester, being careful not
rate white portion which is bitter. Zest is
referred to as grated peel in recipes.

TENING BUTTER OR MARGARINE

o soften 1 stick of butter, remove
pper and place butter on a microwave-
safe plate. Microwave on medium-low
power (30%) 20 to 30 seconds.

SOFTENING CREAM CHEESE

To soften cream cheese, remove wrapper
and place cream cheese on a microwave-
safe plate. Microwave on medium power
(50%) 1 to 1½ minutes for one 8-ounce
package or 30 to 45 seconds for one
3-ounce package.

TOASTING COCONUT

To toast coconut, spread a thin layer of
coconut on an ungreased baking sheet.
Stirring occasionally, bake 5 to 7 minutes in
a 350-degree oven until coconut is light
brown.

EQUIVALENT MEASUREMENTS

1 tablespoon	=	3 teaspoons
⅛ cup (1 fluid ounce)	=	2 tablespoons
¼ cup (2 fluid ounces)	=	4 tablespoons
⅓ cup	=	5⅓ tablespoons
½ cup (4 fluid ounces)	=	8 tablespoons
¾ cup (6 fluid ounces)	=	12 tablespoons
1 cup (8 fluid ounces)	=	16 tablespoons or ½ pint
2 cups (16 fluid ounces)	=	1 pint
1 quart (32 fluid ounces)	=	2 pints
½ gallon (64 fluid ounces)	=	2 quarts
1 gallon (128 fluid ounces)	=	4 quarts

HELPFUL FOOD EQUIVALENTS

½ cup butter	=	1 stick butter
1 square baking chocolate	=	1 ounce chocolate
1 cup chocolate chips	=	6 ounces chocolate chips
2¼ cups packed brown sugar	=	1 pound brown sugar
3½ cups unsifted confectioners sugar	=	1 pound confectioners sugar
2 cups granulated sugar	=	1 pound granulated sugar
4 cups all-purpose flour	=	1 pound all-purpose flour

RECIPE INDEX

CREDITS

To Magna IV Color Imaging of Little Rock, Arkansas, we say thank you for the superb color reproduction and excellent pre-pr preparation.

We want to especially thank photographers Mark Mathews, Larry Pennington, Karen Shirey, and Ken West of Peerl Photography, Little Rock, Arkansas, and Jerry R. Davis of Jerry Davis Photography, Little Rock, Arkansas, for their time, patience, excellent work.